BLUE MOUNTAIN MIST

PART OF THE EVOLVING SERIES

YILDIZ ILKIN

Library and Archives Canada
Library and Archives Canada Cataloguing in Publication
A record for this title (2015) is available from Library & Archives Canada.

Balboa Press books may be ordered through booksellers or by contacting:

Balboa Press
A Division of Hay House
1663 Liberty Drive
Bloomington, IN 47403
www.balboapress.com
1 (877) 407-4847

Print information available on the last page.

ISBN: 978-1-5043-6223-8 (sc)
ISBN: 978-1-5043-6224-5 (e)

Balboa Press rev. date: 11/03/2016

BALBOA
PRESS
A DIVISION OF HAY HOUSE

The Wings Of Freedom
Kanat

In this age when the moral superiority of a particular culture is determined on the basis of its capacity to render nations powerful. Laws, ethics, educations will remain supreme to all beings. Our world, should now become our push towards social betterment. This book is dedicated to my two shamanic looking children: Teymor and Kar Shane Lee Hing. And the study to be presented of our indigenous people's historical development globally to that of an attempt or highlight in rectifying problems on land.

By Author Yildiz Ilkin

Author's Foreword

Once upon a time a handful roamed and started labelling the planet.

They became our global heritage and legacy. The Ottoman- Kanata unravel began with an ironic twist of faith and the going of backwards regarding an in-depth look at the analysis of the start of life. The historic story of "Shaman Was Thy Name" is how it commenced. Our human timeline, not to be confused with medicine doctors or priests. Its human developmental journey of prior to 10,000BC is our focus today.

The truth is the globe is changing and the speed of information is more readily accessible. One would think the pushing of advancement was easy in the 21ˢᵗ Century, not so this author learned the hard way. Luckily, Canada proved to be an even greater country! In historical timelines however, it is still relatively new to the rest of the world, which in turned made the launch of the several publications questionable in presentation globally. The content was so heavy academics were hesitant on how other countries would react.

The battle of the century had started between different countries, their political agendas, the flow of information, the shakeup of religion and one author's legal democratic right. I paid heavily for the separation of academics from politics, challenging continuously those who protect for being confined and the bright light that came on regarding humanities global history.

In the dark the questions posed to me were is this a mental breakdown, has someone done something to you, are you a foreign spy or some type of sophisticated android. Yildiz it is the irregularities of what has happened to you and the religious component! What do we tell other world leaders and many in the public who are so science based? We absolutely can't bring all of this out.

"Ever heard of luck," was my answer or winning the one in seven billion lotto? I swear the following is true it is my background, sensory intelligence or maybe Divine. In the end the concept of progressive thought somewhat won and the rest of my work you can bring out 100 years from now when everything has cooled down was my blatantly cocky response. Cant a human diverge into several different areas without sustaining further injury?

Furthermore, by pushing academia and merging topics like linguistics, anthropology, higher spirituality, social behaviors and our environment's role, we are able to develop as humans. Our goal ultimately is promoting a different cognitive thought process in pushing evolving to a whole new frontier. One with a global progressive vision for advancing.

One aspect of the research presented was the field of linguistic anthropology. A new type of academia which is defined as the concept of analyzing languages first based on its chronology of order, then extracting these words for anthropological use. I merged one part of my professional career of being a legal abstracter with my years of hobby research. To make simple, this dissecting aides us in looking at first dialogues more closely and in collecting material by the use of their descriptive narratives. A very simple mode or attempt to assess how primitive man first saw the world or started their various evolutionary excursions.

Yes we have found a treasure box full of jewels in certain regions of the world for anthropology. It is these narratives that were critical in the study of early human social behaviors leading up to one person's vision of how we have not fully reached optimum levels of advancement.

The attempt to understand radicalization of global languages, to that of what is human self-preservation and behavioral dynamics. These actions are merged with the basic functionality of economics and their vital roles in pushing progress. The question now is how do we attempt to create a state of equilibrium or what is healthy sustainability while comparing it to what went wrong historically?

Human advancement will be presented as the final periodical- called "Let's Evolve". These series will be a set of projected proposals of urban/ rural layout and pilot projects followed with ideas on progressive environmentalism at what should be its ecosystem balance levels. What I call the basics of actually implementing our utopic world. The capacity to blend existence within earth's wall in a more maintainable way. Blue Mountain Mist starts this voyage. Its extraction studies many probable areas of shamanic dialogues - to later on deduce what went wrong historically. Almost like a Nostradamus forthcoming using a multi-faceted background, a higher sensory and some years of ESL education.

Starting with shamanism as a connector point to all humans found globally and why humanity created such detrimental distinctions amongst themselves. The parity of the human race. These poems link countries so that we can push progress. The final stage being the field of social studies under the umbrella, called "social betterment".

One that encompassing all the historical taboo out there starting with: what was a shaman, why was the culture of shaman hidden historically (yes there was a culture), the role of linguistics to religion and lastly breaking human perceptions in pushing the new dynamics of environmental thinking will now be our mandate?

Putting politics aside and marketing our connections as humans in pushing green using my discovery of Kanata's broader meaning of Wings Cover (versus settlement) on July 1st, 2013.

These seven other successions presented below: are called a different voice of reason or thinking. Presenting in series format the evolution of Human to Humanoid will be featured in series format.

a) Animal To Hominid
b) The Language Of Birds
c) The Shamanic History Of Kanat
d) The Venus Conversion
e) Let's Evolve
f) Unravelling The Impacts Of Foreign Intelligence in the Middle East

The future will be known as the "enlightenment" of the Kanata-Ottoman unravel. With the hopes of pushing the practicality of a female's thought process and creative thinking to that of a better world. Called a planet in the healing, our power call:

Enjoy, Yildiz Ilkin

A Canadian Heritage Poem

Kanada Tribe, Is This All Your Home?

We land on this land, ice
everywhere, it's 1534.
Do you think they will like us?
Indian what is your name?

They don't answer. Keep
trying, they still don't answer.
I tell them mine.
Europe told us they are the
Kana people.

I think they are from Kana'da
tribe. Indian where is your
home?

We pretend to do sleeping.
The land is cold; our men
are ghastly sick.
We need food, danger lurks
around us.

They point and say, "Kanat',
Kanat'ta".
It looks like a small
settlement.

We travel up north.
There are a hundred more,
Indian where are all of you from?

Iroquois, Hochelaga, Algonquin.
We must make way.
Europe is famished,
our people are hit with a plague.
We are so cold.

Our history says ugly,
we too have tribes and
protect our own.

But tomorrow when we
get stronger, we will make way.

Yildiz Ilkin

*The term Kana'da gives us an alternative
explanation on the etymology of Canada's
name derivative. See webpage www.
starilkin.com for additional notes.*

Content

Section A

Section B

Name Of Country	Official Regional Title	Poem Title	Code ID	Page Number
Bahamas	The Commonwealth Of The Bahamas	Baby Blue Crystal Glass	B1	23
Bahrain	The Kingdom Of Bahrain	Meaningful Female	B2	24
Bangladesh	People's Republic Of Bangladesh	Bengal Tiger	B3	25
Barbados	Barbados	The Little Boy And His Bridge	B4	26
Belarus	Republic Of Belarus	The Beloved Aya	B5	27
Belgium	Kingdom Of Belgium	How God's Tears Made The Rivers	B6	28
Belize	Belize	Dear Spirits	B7	29
Benin	The Republic Of Benin	Spirits Of Africa	B8	30
Bhutan	The Kingdom Of Bhutan	Clean Spirited Soul	B9	31
Bolivia	Republic Of Bolivia	The Landing Point Tiwanaku	B10	32
Bonaire	Kingdom's Island Of Bonaire	See: Finding Heaven Underneath	A19	19
Bosnia And Herzegovina	Republic Of Bosnia And Herzegovina	Mehmet Pasha	B11	33
Botswana	The Republic Of Botswana	Running Free With The Herd	B12	34
Brazil	Brazil	Pink River Dolphin	B13	35
Brunei	Brunei Darussalam	Sultanate	B14	36
Bulgaria	Republic Of Bulgaria	Proverb	B15	36
	Republic Of Bulgaria	God's Gift	B16	37
	Republic Of Bulgaria	See: Beyond The River Evros	H4	114
Burkina Faso	Burkina Faso	A World Once Before	B17	38
Burundi	The Republic Of Burundi	The Mountains	B18	39

Section C

Name Of Country	Official Regional Title	Poem Title	Code ID	Page Number
Cambodia	The Kingdom Of Cambodia	Angkor	C1	40
Cameroon	The Republic Of Cameroon	Wah-za National Park	C2	41
Canada	Canada	Patriotic Heart	C3	41
	Canada	Canada's New Skyline	C4	42
	Canada	I Stole The Apple From The Bee	C5	43
	Canada	Shaman Was My Name	C6	44
	Canada	The Bering Confusion	C7	46
	Canada	Turkish Girl	C8	48
	Canada	White Negro Child	C9	49
	Canada	C'est La Vie	C10	50
	Canada	What Has The Blues Given	C11	51
Cape Verde	The Republic Of Cape Verde	The Isles Off Africa	C12	52
Central African Republic	The Central African Republic	Chari River	C13	53
Central Asia	Central Asia	The Shamanic Prayer	C14	54
	Central Asia	The Stan's Of Central Asia	C15	55
	Central Asia	See: Battle After Battle, They Became	A6	5
Chad	The Republic Of Chad	Quilted Tapestry	C16	56
Chile	Republic Of Chile	The Black Mummy	C17	57
China	The People's Republic Of China	Peking Man	C18	58
	The People's Republic Of China	Dark Fairy Mountains	C19	59
	The People's Republic Of China	Proverb	C20	59
	The People's Republic Of China	Your Majesty	C21	60
Clans of Southern Turkey	Region Clans OF Southern Turkey	Blue Eyes	C22	61
Colombia	The Republic Of Colombia	By The Railway	C23	62
Comoros	The Union Of The Comoros	The Essence Of Vanilla	C24	63

Congo, Democratic Republic	The Democratic Republic Of The Congo	Congo's Genocide	C25	64
Congo, Republic The	People's Republic Of Congo	Teke, The Minority Is This Tribe	C26	65
Costa Rica	The Republic Of Costa Rica	Tropical Nights	C27	66
Cote D'Ivoire	The Republic Of Cote D'Ivoire	Pygmy Hippopotamus	C28	67
Croatia	Republic Of Croatia	Wild Horse	C29	68
Cuba	The Republic Of Cuba	Oh How I Love The Cuban People	C30	69
Curacao	Curacao (2005)	See: Finding Heaven Underneath	A19	19
Cyprus	The Republic Of Cyprus	Run My Loved Ones	C31	70
Czech Republic	Czech Republic	The Halo	C32	71

Section D

Name Of Country	Official Regional Title	Poem Title	Code ID	Page Number
Denmark	Kingdom Of Denmark	The Cultural Touch	D1	72
	Kingdom Of Denmark	The Nissum Fjord	D2	73
Djibouti	The Republic Of Djibouti	The Market In Djibouti	D3	74
Dominica	Commonwealth Of Dominica	Boiling Lake	D4	74
Dominican Republic	The Dominican Republic	War Of Independence	D5	75

Section E

Name Of Country	Official Regional Title	Poem Title	Code ID	Page Number
Ecuador	Republic Of Ecuador	Almost Human	E1	76
Egypt	Arab Republic Of Egypt	The Spirit Of Tutankhamen	E2	77
	Arab Republic Of Egypt	The Warrior Known As Musa	E3	78
El Salvador	The Republic Of El Salvador	Spectrum Of Light	E4	79
Equatorial Guinea	The Republic Of Equatorial Guinea	The Fang Chief Said	E5	80
Eritrea	Eritrea	The Admiration Of Aksumite Empire	E6	80
Estonia	Republic Of Estonia	The Transformation of Tallinn	E7	81

Ghana	The Republic Of Ghana	The Struggle Of Women	G6	97
	The Republic Of Ghana	See: Slave Route	A13	12
Global	Global	Earth Became My Zoo	G7	98
	Global	A Secret	G8	99
	Global	I Grip Your Head Tight	G9	49
	Global	Whose Monkey Is The Better Monkey?	G10	101
Greece	The Hellenic Republic	The Greek Goddess	G11	102
	The Hellenic Republic	Konyaliyim	G12	103
	The Hellenic Republic	The Skatan	G13	103
	The Hellenic Republic	A Mix of Three, We Became Thee	G14	104
Greenland	Greenland	The Fight For Artic	G15	105
Grenada	Grenada	New Granada	G16	106
Guam	Guam	Chukchi Nomads Of Guam	G17	57
Guatemala	The Republic Of Guatemala	I Love God	G18	107
Guinea	The Republic Of Guinea	Guinea Fowl	G19	108
Guinea- Bissau	The Republic Of Guinea-Bissau	Traditional African Religion	G20	109
Guyana	Co-operative Republic Of Guyana	Sleep Peacefully Mama	G21	110

Section H

Name Of Country	Official Regional Title	Poem Title	Code ID	Page Number
Haiti	The Republic Of Haiti	The Red Voodoo	H1	112
	The Republic Of Haiti	Proverb	H2	112
Hattusa, Hittite Empire	Territory	The Secret Lines	H3	113
Hebrus River, Surroundings	Territory	Beyond The River Hebrus	H4	114
Honduras, Barbados, Panama	The Republic Of Honduras	Captain Sir Henry Morgan	H5	115
Hungary	Republic Of Hungary	Counting Sheep	H6	116

Section I

Name Of Country	Official Regional Title	Poem Title	Code ID	Page Number
Iceland	The Republic Of Iceland	The Dolls Of Iceland	I1	117
India	Republic Of India	Ram Is My Kar	I2	118
	Republic Of India	The Revolution	I3	119
	Republic Of India	Sanskrit	I4	119
	Republic Of India	Ignore Monogamy	I5	120
	Republic Of India	Sun Temple Konarak	I6	120
	Republic Of India	See: Hindu Kush	P1	184
Indonesia	Republic Of Indonesia	The Living	I7	121
Iran	The Islamic Republic Of Iran	Assassin	I8	122
	The Islamic Republic Of Iran	The Three Prayers And One Sacrifice of Elam	I9	123
Iraq	Republic Of Iraq	Feeding The Sun God	I10	117
	Republic Of Iraq	Ottoman Head Quarters	I11	125
	Republic Of Iraq	Tribal We Are	I12	126
	Republic Of Iraq	Uri	I13	127
Ireland	Eire (Republic Of Ireland)	Castle On Inishmore	I14	128
Israel	The State Of Israel	Adam or …..	I15	129
	The State Of Israel	Ahu'di	I16	130
	The State Of Israel	The Elder of Safad	I17	131
	The State Of Israel	The White Lion Of Golan Heights	I18	132
	The State Of Israel	Yehudi	I19	133
	The State Of Israel	The Seven Day War	I20	134
	The State Of Israel	See: The Warrior Known As Musa	E3	78
	The State Of Israel	See: Homage to Yacoub Aġa	L7	149
Italy	The Republic Of Italy	Marco Polo	I21	126
	The Republic Of Italy	Roma's Mark	I22	136
	The Republic Of Italy	See: Columbus Said	S26	218

Section J

Name Of Country	Official Regional Title	Poem Title	Code ID	Page Number
Jamaica	Jamaica	Proverb	J1	137
	Jamaica	Bob Marley	J2	137
Japan	Japan	Osaka	J3	137

	Japan	Shintoism	J4	137
Jordan	The Hashemite Kingdom Of Jordan	Dry River Valley	J5	138

Section K

Name Of Country	Official Regional Title	Poem Title	Code ID	Page Number
Kazakhstan	Republic Of Kazakhstan	Dark Wings, Black Nights	K1	139
Kenya	The Republic Of Kenya	Hours Spent Studying Fingers And Skies	K2	140
Kiribati	Republic Of Kirbati	Magical Phoenix	K3	141
Kosovo	Kosovo	The Ova Of Birds	K4	141
Kuwait	State Of Kuwait	Tragedy Of Life	K5	142
Kyrgyzstan	Republic Of Kyrgyzstan	The Poet	K6	143

Section L

Name Of Country	Official Regional Title	Poem Title	Code ID	Page Number
Laos	Lao People's Democratic Republic	The One Million Elephants	L1	144
Latvia	Republic Of Latvia	Walk Along With Me	L2	145
Lebanon	The Republic Of Lebanon	Roman Style	L3	146
Lesotho	Lesotho	What Is Death	L4	147
Liberia	The Republic Of Liberia	Graveyard	L5	147
Libya	The Socialist People's Libyan Arab Jumhuriya	Tour Guide To Tourist	L6	148
Libya to Ukraine	The Historical Coastal Line Walkway	Homage to Yacoub Aġa	L7	149
Liechtenstein	Principality Of Liechtenstein	Liechtenstein	L8	150
Lithuania	Republic Of Lithuania	Follow The Path Of Light	L9	150
Luxembourg	Grand Duchy Of Luxembourg	House Of Burgundy	L10	151

Section M

Name Of Country	Official Regional Title	Poem Title	Code ID	Page Number
Macedonia	The Former Yugoslav Republic Of Macedonia	In Search Of Sanctuary	M1	152

Samoa	The Independent State Of Samoa	Tutuila	S5	202
San Marino	The Most Serene Republic Of San Marino	Ave Maria	S6	218
Sao Tome And Principe	The Democratic Republic Of Sao Tome And Principe	The Land Made Me	S7	203
Saudi Arabia	Kingdom Of Saudi Arabia	We Apologize	S8	204
Scandinavian Countries - South Africa to The Sahara Belt	Territories	In The Battle Of Life	S9	205
	Territories	In The Battle Of Life	S10	206
Senegal	The Republic Of Senegal	Dances of Life	S11	207
Serbia	Republic Of Serbia	Stari Ras	S12	208
Seychelles	Republic Of Sychelles	Historical	S13	208
Sierra Leone	The Republic Of Sierra Leone	Raven's In The Sky	S14	209
Singapore	Republic Of Singapore	My Motto Is Balance	S15	210
	Republic Of Singapore	Our Indian Prince	S16	211
Slovakia	Slovak Republic	Is There A God?	S17	212
Slovenia	Republic Of Slovenia	The Stilt Houses Of Slovenia	S18	212
Solomon Islands	Soloman Islands	Darkness	S19	212
Somalia	Somalia	Shaman You Are, Shaman I am	S20	213
South Africa	Republic Of South Africa	In the Light Of The Sun	S21	214
	Republic Of South Africa	See: The Beauty Of Raw	N1	168
	Republic Of South Africa	See: In the Battle Of Life	S3	201
	Republic Of South Africa	See: In The Battle Of Life	S9	205
South Korea	The Republic Of Korea	Many Moons Ago	S22	215
South Sudan	South Sudan	Historical	S23	215
Spain	The Kingdom Of Spain	The Sons Of Darkness	S24	216
	The Kingdom Of Spain	Ci or Si or Sea?	S25	217
	The Kingdom Of Spain	Columbus Said	S26	218
Sri Lanka	The Democratic Socialist Republic Of Sri Lanka	The Flying Goddess	S27	219
Sudan	Republic Of Sudan	They Asked Nubia	S28	220
Suriname	The Republic Of Suriname	Historical	S29	220
Swaziland	The Kingdom Of Swaziland	The Great River Of Usutu	S30	221

Section T

Section U

Name Of Country	Official Regional Title	Poem Title	Code ID	Page Number
Uganda	The Republic Of Uganda	The Gods	U1	241
Ukraine	Ukraine	Titanium	U2	242
	Ukraine	See: Homage to Yacoub Aġa	L7	149
United Arab Emirates	United Arab Emirates	Evil Spirits	U3	243
United Kingdom	United Kingdom Of Great Britain And Northern Ireland	Evolutionary Difficulties	U4	244
	United Kingdom Of Great Britain And Northern Ireland	The Lady With The Lamp	U5	245
	United Kingdom Of Great Britain And Northern Ireland	The Light Of Europe	U6	246
	United Kingdom Of Great Britain And Northern Ireland	Historical	U7	246
United States	United States Of America	Alpha Quadrant	U8	247
	United States Of America	Kokopelli Tribe	U9	248
	United States Of America	The Other Side Of War	U10	249
	United States Of America	Stuck At The Border	U11	250
	United States Of America	Apache	U12	250
United States, New York	United States Of America	Manhattan	U13	251
United States, Los Angeles	United States Of America	I Am The Fallen Angel Lucifer	U14	252
Uruguay	The Oriental Republic Of Uruguay	The Poisonous Shells	U15	252
Uzbekistan	The Republic Of Uzbekistan	The Moon In The Day	U16	253

Section V

Name Of Country	Official Regional Title	Poem Title	Code ID	Page Number
Vanuatu	The Republic Of Vanuatu	Roi Mata	V1	254
Vatican City	The State OF The Vatican City aka The Holy See	Homage To The Sky	V2	254
Venezuela	The Bolivarian Republic Of Venezuela	Caracas	V3	255
Vietnam	The Socialist Republic Of Vietnam	Listen Only To Your Inner Soul	V4	256

Section Y

Name Of Country	Official Regional Title	Poem Title	Code ID	Page Number
Yemen	Republic Of Yemen	Al- Yaman	Y1	257

Section Z

Name Of Country	Official Regional Title	Poem Title	Code ID	Page Number
Zambia	The Republic Of Zambia	The Highest	Z1	258
Zimbabwe	The Republic Of Zimbabwe	Kariba	Z2	259

Acknowledgements

The Heavens And My Soul

Bămiăn Valley

We lost another artefact,
tears we cry today.
A Buddhist monastic
symbol.

Heritage early man
so easily for took.
Not understanding
the prayers it laid.

And how lively and
commerce filled
the region was when
Western Turks
and Genghis Khan
once ruled.

Part of our shamanic
Gandhara art.
Gone are the hands that
took hours to make.

Massive mountains carved
one millimeter at a time.
The century of chisel by
primitively sharpened tools.

When earth becomes fully human,
we will build it again one day.

*Visualize Chiseling, The Mountainside
2650 Years Ago.*

A2- Afghanistan

We are managed by the Persian Achaemenian Empire and have just met the wrath of Alexander the Great.	*How Interlinked All Humans Are Today*

A3- Africa

We Say Ruh!

We bang hard on his chest
Ruh

He is not coming back
Ruh
We mourn around him
Ruh
We shake our heads
Ruh
Hear our animal sounds
Ruh

We now understand he is with
the ones flying.

Coming from the land of dark
spirits.

Ruh they once had said.

Adorned by their masks, and straw dresses.

Where proto-Turkic Afrikaans known as one part of our global shamanic linguistic history out of Africa was born.

*Look Carefully I Told Them,
At The Hand Of An Ape*

Balkan Traveler

Balkan regional friend.
You come tired to this
town called Berat.

Part of your Ottoman heritage too.
It speaks to us about
the many things we
may have missed of our past.

Vacant it sits alone,
on this very mountain top.
How our early humans
prayed, where it now stands.

The 13th-century citadel,
that is tall and protected today.
A designed so typically the same
to that of its era.

First floors were for the freezing
cold months they huddled.
The second floor for the breezy
love making of the summers
that once had slipped by.

Balkan traveler stand very still
and quiet, in this old kule.
And listen carefully to those like you
who once had passed by.

*I Drew This Picture Of The Berat
and Gjirokastra Centre*

A5- Algeria

Kasbah of Algeria

The many worlds of Africa,
exotic and ancient.

Centuries of ancestors ago.
Bâh, our shamans, would first
attempt to make vocal for cover.

Our earliest designated feeding points.
The fierce power and muscle;
they called the region of the
many Gods who stole lives.

Phoenician trading posts,
their temporary resting place.
Evolved it to become
the center point of
protected town living.

Ottoman style palaces
became transformed again.
A deeply rooted community,
of honour and Islamic teachings.

Kasbah your winding streets
and ancient alleys.

Made this medina one of North Africa
finest civilizations of life.

Once Had The Waterfalls Of Life

Battle After Battle, They Became

The Byzantine Splendour
Christian, Muslim, Jew we house all!
From North Africa to Persia we reach.
Accept our lead and save life.
Gold, you must pay.
We will not pull a strife.

The Mongolian Empire Monarchs
Earthly shamanic spirits we are,
to Ankara we reach.
Accept our empire and save life.
Feed us, you must pay.
Understand our severest of ways.

The Ottoman Grandeur
Christian, Muslim, Jew and more,
we all are.
Forty-two territories we reach.
Accept us and save life.
Honour us, or death will be your fate.

This is a must for each one of us;
understand our bond and unity.
We stand tall.

The Range of Byzantine Empire

The Rabbi And His Goose

The Rabbi with his rosy red cheeks,
on the way to the open market
near Balat found an injured
baby goose.

Come home with me.
Let me feed you something to eat,
and help you fix your injury.

But first let's take five minutes
to sit away from this dreadful heat.
The flowing water by the stream
will cool both of us down
while I check everything.

You can roam in our garden
and I do love animals do not fear.
Just provide some eggs
and we will make sure other
animals stay clear.

The white goose that day onward
followed the Rabbi everywhere he went.

The Rabbi And His Goose
An Anatolian Tale

Spain's Persecution

Hear ye, Hear ye
Oh great Sultan,
they desperately need your
help.

The message was read.
The year is 1453,
Spain is after us.
Torn are our shoes,
barefoot we wail.

Send the ships
immediately.
Hardship looms over
the many, their message
echoes through.

The harbour boats,
they wait.
One at a time they arrive,
thousands of nautical miles
from home.

"You stay with us", the Ottoman's say,
Born were you from our regions,
you belong to us Yerusha people.

Filled with honour like us,
let those find God,
who harm you.

"You can trade and will find peace in our
regions".

The Ottomans, once had said.

*Ottoman ships picking up Jews in Spain in
1453, also known as the historical expulsion
of Jews.*

Two Goats On A Bridge

Elders would tell many
stories to teach the young.
Here is another that was,
happily, sung.

Two goats attempted to
cross the narrow bridge.
Both said move,
so I can have first dibs.

Both bleated as they fought
and headed each other.
Together they fell off and
died in a fretted mutter.

The moral of the story
is simple you see!

While we bicker about
our shamanic history
and the dialogues of
our first.

Earth is missing a lot
especially in quenching thirst.

Being the wisest of the wise,
we can use our Native ideologies.
The discovery of wings to push
progress and be utterly green.

The lessons of these goats
should now be remembered
by us historically.

Politics is politics but
academia always comes first.

Unlike the other two goats
in the fable, pretty equal in size.

If you don't see the rays
coming through Academia;
our prism of sky blue lights
as brighter.

Even with political disguise,
we may all fall off and die.

Surrender please and move aside.

Historic Fables Of The Region

The Princess Who Marked Her Name

Our forefathers once lived
in early darkness,
in animal hide tents.

At the base of the mountains
they would lean up against
the large boulders to naturally
protect against those that caused cold.

They would ask the highest,
Anie Peak.
Give us another story.
The feminine spirit would gently
respond back.

Of how Pyrene the mighty,
gave birth to a serpent.
And she would then run away
into the woods.

Afraid that her father, the earthly giant
would be angry.
Alone, she would pour out her heartfelt
story to the trees and their surroundings.
But this time attracting the attention of wild
beasts who tore her to pieces.

Are you afraid our forefathers would ask?
Only to find the children had
quickly fallen asleep.

Snuggled five in a row, under heavy pounds
of leathery-fur pull. The only item to protect
against dreadful colds.

The covers neatly scraped and washed with palm
comfortable rocks. The passing of time our early
humans first attempted to do.

In the agonizing months of subzero cold
and a human resilient will, to simply get through.

The Princess Pyrene

The Lion And The Bird

Landscape saturation over time
means a relationship.
Our ecosystems even developed
species variant, animal friendships.

The little bird one day pecked
at the lion's rear in his territory
at the base of the river basin
Okavango.

The lion looked ferociously;
this bird must be insane
and giggled what the hell
is this near?

Something went funny
he got a peck more.
But enjoyed the kiss of the
unwanted host that rode.

Like the hippo and the crocodile,
they too became inseparable mates.

This is a story of politics we know
is a hidden secret using the case
of the lion and his little mate.

The King Of The Jungle

Irishmen We Are

Ulster was our region,
back home.

The wild wolf and the stars
symbolized where we came from.

In 1688, we came to
Anguilla and just took.

An empty acre of flat land,
was the scene
where our shamrocks still
can be found.

The sound of ocean tides every time
the wind blew, made it an awesome
living ground!

Its coral and limestone
reflects are new spirits.

Irish we are but
Anguilla became our
second home.

The Irishmen In Anguilla!

A13- Antigua and Barbuda

Slave Route

Africa has no history, no memory no castles or forts. As far as we are concern they don't even have humans.

The captain spoke. The death ships arrived one by one. Their history was to become known as the emergence of fire.

The earliest chronicles of Antiguan abhorrence to the injustices of faith. The slashing of raw flesh on barb wire.

The Amerindians first hesitantly came to shore, they presented a circle in a flat chiseled marked stone.

Life, silence, sharing, respect it showed. Our tribes give it to those we encounter first. Their attempt to be pleasantly bold.
Flipped off their hands the foreigners did. Our historical past tells us of the injured spirits that once were the same scenes overseas.

But some islands became uniquely hated, by the masters themselves. This history dictates to us so very well.

Antigua is one, with a majestic sounding of conch horn, to alarm all the bells.

They were the blood of Ghana Warriors these slaves rebelled continuously.

The island that now became known as the beautiful picturesque 14-mile zone from hell. At first conquest, something interesting history hides from others, this must be told.

Slaves and island inhabitant through base understanding became the wild barbarians, that first became unified against all their foes.

Drastically sick became the locals and the first to go. Their spirits back those at war. But it was the negro who endured the longest torment and torture.

The bone grinder it was known did not persuade differently any of their anguish and despair. We will turn this entire island into a fortress the nightly private talks were held.

We will exterminate all white population that comes.

We are not like the others; their grunting can still be heard echoing through the tide's swell.

<u>*Continue*</u>

"Ghana Chiefs"
They pounded heavily on their chest!
Ocean salt, mixed blood with sweat.
That heavily came down.
Proud is the blood of our
ancestry we carry.
Death till we are free!
We will never have any boundaries.

They circled barefoot with sticks, the island sandy floor. Holding it against the inevitable counterattack, island visits started to slow.

Antigua to be remembered by its proud Amerindian, slave rebellion name.

The earliest visuals of labeling, what was a foreign revelation, of utmost misery.

The Breaking Of Human Locks

How Spoiled We Are

Many things in this world we take for granted!
Voltage power, running tap
water and our high towers.

For many centuries,
a toilet was the left side of the creek.

What we called a tributary water outlet.
The settling of early humans
in-between a vee.

Where one side became to eat and
the other side became the raw hand
of a wipe and to leak.

The grounds were dug, four feet deep.
And animals were put
in a circular position where they
could all sleep.

When the mountain's whistled
and temperatures fell at -40 below.
The story changed to struggle
and the unbearableness of the
extremity of no heat.

Something fascinating happened, part of our
animal kingdom narration of an environmental
scuffle.

Early humans to prevent freezing
slept in the middle of their
herded cattle.

This bond with our living
became part of our survival huddle.
The animal breath and the smell
of feces did not matter.

The life of human became what is creative
endurance. The story of, are we going
to exist one more day; the surroundings,
became humanities dreadful rival.

Integrated we are with the living.
Little do we know how hard it
was for early human survival.

*An old Armenian village creatively designed and
placed westerly-wind protected on a mountain
side, was part of an independent kingdom known
as Vannad.*

She Was Made In Ararat

Made were you in bliss but
the souls of her past were
imprinted onto her mother's
womb even before she was born.

The conception that became a
life lasting of sensory of pain.
One that held her purpose
with the dawning of each light.
The transfer of the forgotten,
called the spirit of past ghosts.

The mountains centuries old,
were always known by her
forefathers as lethal in disguise.

For every tear, that existed on its slopes
suffering transformed her.
A wretched mark on her soul.
The hiding points known as the
peaks of aches.

The once lethal summits
nowadays simply lights up at
its base, with a glimmer of hope.

Our ancestry is the highlight.
Many changes have been made.
But the mountains of pain,
are still its famous name.

We will gaze and chant for hours at its lethal peaks, this historic church was placed overlooking our Ararat mountains.

Our Elder Female

Your beautiful skin
untold by the marks
of life.

Even when you scratch
your face,
to show others
the immense pain
of an incident unfolded.

A womb ripped with
shreds of sweat.
You are proud of your age
showing all your beautiful
grey tussles.

Refusing even root dye or
henna.
The realism of a genuine woman;
indigenous and proud yet
never forgotten.

As an elder female,
you have a different spiritual role
one for the protection of giving life and
in helping to change the future.

You have given your life
for those up to seven generations
after you.

Elder Female

Family We Became

Almond shape are our eyes,
a beautiful light bronze was
our skin.

They once quietly said,
You are brothers of our men
You are brothers of our men

Pahlavi alphabet resembles that
of the cradle, Ethiopia.
You are brothers of our men
You are brothers of our men

We permanently mark our women,
for decor. We too are shamanic, by surprise.
You are brothers of our men
You are brothers of our men

Forefathers of Bizan, Hurrian, Ottoman and the
many before us
became our ancestral pride.

The tribes which made the fabric of us.
Culture is our heritage, the existence that became
ingrained in trust.

We now happily sing.
Mother first, you made all of us.
The human spirit, our prayers, which
made it our Hayrana.

We now understand life, our tribes
from within, one of our oldest even
recorded by Damascus first.

We acknowledge today, we are really only
Brothers of your men.
Brothers of your men.

Armenian Indigenous People- Nubarian
Library Paris, found online, Open to All....

The Ova Of Crosses

Southern Turkey, contains a dark secret.
The bodies of thousands.
Quietly buried but not forgotten.
Call it our gruesome past.

Some say Ottoman infractions,
the other half,
yells "blatant murder and a
systematically ghastliest task".

The harshest decisions
parents had to make.
"Give us some of your ancestry
or all of you die at the stake".

To appease the local women
who wailed, leave the innocence please.
Many children, each family took.
Young girls were married off quick.

One by one, the Ova of crosses represented
the life given back to earth.

Of the regions, they once called heritage.
A genocide of war, and a no-mercy on the human
core.

A shatter of a heart shaped glass.
The study of many atrocities
should make humanity think
about our past.

How empty the meaning of life.

Does it really matter,
the change we can't revive?
What went wrong and the
life that disappeared?

We should all say, *"examine these early human*
atrocities and push human consciousness to the
level of extreme."

This is humanities new social ethics and the
remembrance of the spirits that were
once seen.

The Ova Of Crosses

Finding Heaven Underneath

A small crack of sunlight
in the sky, amongst the clouds.
On the boat I stand.
The salt water touches
my lips.

Captain which point will
you stop?
A few nautical miles south,
of Belafonte's Isle.
He smiles.

At first doesn't seem like
much.
But mermaid I be.
Jump nude in the water
what a sight, I now see?

Blue parrot fishes,
corals made of
pinks, silvers, and metallic
greens.

The many years of edging knife,
what I call this earth's injury upon me.

I healed my wounds that day,
when I literally found heaven
in all the ocean life underneath.

Our Marine Life

A20- Australia

The Male Organ

The male organ was born from
a parasite on this large island shore.
Evolved over thousands of years
and numerous shapes.

Its head reared by the mere
fabric of earth.
A design some feverishly
argue was coincidental made
only from ape.

Hosts and predators
their social behaviors
in our ecosystems became
naturally built.

Our world was moulded
from such an interactive
living display; an astonishing
patch work of quilt!

Centuries later the bringing
up of light; transformed itself
into the study of human design.

In the end, regardless of human logic,
these malformations had to
have been aided by the skies.

Call it Awa, Hava or Eve,
stork, big bang theory

or miracle formation.
Its conception was one of a kind!

Parasitic is the highlight,
what was called transforming
into the better of evolve.

The Parasitic Redesigned
That Needed Energy

A21- Australia

Amata

Child born were you from the womb
that germinated from this soil.

Everything about you is made from this *black earth*.

Earth's Keeper I am

The woman in me,
an extension of soil.
The early Amadeus of the
first songs of the Ravens
that flew high.

Earth's keeper I am
locked in these mountains.
The view of the Wachau's
landscape.
Our hands scabbed,
by the difficulties of terrain.

Our calves are a
mere trunk of a tree that
extends upwards
and waves freely in
the skies.

Earth's keeper I am.
Still existing in spirit.
Connect us as one soul today.

The Super-Organism Called Earth

A23- Azerbaijan

The Elements of Fire

Long ago, life was really
hard for our first humans.
Hell was earth.

Scorned with hate many were for
all the suffering in place,
they endured.

Walked barefoot we did.
How the clusters on feet
transformed itself to hardened
orangey-calluses.

Omens of our past found
deep, in Azikh's cave.
Nightmares from the
spawns of depth.
Their sacred bones of our past
neatly buried.

Amplified were the pain
of our lives.
Some days, feelings of our
internals, being burnt alive.
Some basics just didn't last.

Others will always remain
the incorporated emotions of
first people of earth,
who used the first elements
as controlled fire.

The Earth And Fire

— B —

Baby Blue Crystal Glass

Baby blue are the waters
from the hilltop we can
see right through
the ocean floor.

Another one lost
say a group of Lukayan.
All we see are the tips
that glide through.

Emotionless they stand
still, to watch the diving pelikans
eat the departed remains.

Their voices of fear,
we can still feel through
the breeze.

We ask the skies,
please can you just
leave us alone.

Give us some food they wailed,
and let these evil spirts
of land and sea
be gone.

The Bahamian Emblem

B2- Bahrain

Meaningful Female

Everything living in the
past had a story.
To our meaningful mother;
on the shores they went
to lift their hands to you.

The region for centuries
known as Manama.
O great spirit
tell us more, the heat
from the bonfire would soar.

We decorate the shores
for you.
We put tinsel, leaves and shells.
We even put food to our
ancestry for you.

We light up the skies
with sacred fire.
Through the crackling of blaze
we also pray for the many other
divines like you.

The only existence is darkness.
Through the haze and hours of
circular chants a voice whispers
back to all of them.

Did you hear the one

about the stars and how each one
represents our forefathers?
The biggest one being is Inanna.

She shines every night,
and slides across the heavens.
When people believe in her.

Whisper her name seven times
and look high up.
She will move again for you.
She is the mother that protects
all of your ancestry.

The better place where your forefathers
go, after this planet discomforts you.

The Shooting Star, Inanna

Bengal Tiger

I am great it roared,
the noise even rocked earth.

The mushy waters lining up
Sundarbans mangrove forests.
Where it was happy in its
green tropical home.

No different than these
upright humans.

Gan Chi, the spirit of blood
in my region is exactly
what I am looking for.

A meal to make me stay
very still, for a few days
or more.

A silent predator, I am.
The arrow and bow
are my fierce claws.

The hunt is the only
existence I surely know.

The Bengal Tiger By Ganges

B4- Barbados

The Little Boy And His Bridge

Stories are what teaches,
this one is no different.
This is a tale of a little boy
and his favorite hangout bridge.

One day a truck was crossing,
and couldn't go under the low cover.
Engineers came so quick,
and try to solve this hover.

Confused were many.
More men came in.
We are going to have to tear it
down, this is how we will begin.

The little boy said, *please stop*
can you simply think again!
Fixing can happen, just look at it
from within.

A bridge is a bridge,
don't tear it down please!

This truck is rare and filled
to the brim.
Making it an unusual crease.

Deflate its tires and then it
can cross without being grim.

All men that day
realized something daunting.
When it comes to learning
you can see the light from any.

The Bridgetown Bridge, Of Las Bárbaras

The Beloved Moon, Aya

We think of Europe so
cultivated and advanced.
Once upon a time
they too believed in the forests,
moons and chants.

Bialowieza primeval forest,
how you stand rare
and untouched.
The few left original landscapes
of Europe, what a work
of art by God.

Bison, otter, lynx still litter the
scene.
They tiptoe through the mist and
moved the pine trees to see the
bright moon in between.

The footsteps of human
ancestry when Europe
was green to the spleen.

Their spirits made up souls
of the departed, when the
world just needed food.

Our earliest were known as the cleanest of the
clean.

The European Bison in Belovezhskaya-
Pushcha Forests

How God's Tears Made The Rivers

Blindness fills the people who live
between these shores.

We always feel their spirits.
Koksijde is our shamanic
territorial name;
our first rest, before man
ever settled.

A different native we are, then those
who try to take our home.

Along the channels we fish,
but something has gone wrong.
The heavens, the skies
keeps pouring tears.

So upset the Gods must be.
Their noise and pounding has even
broken all the trees.

Even the land animals run clear.
The deer, the elk, and foxes; the
mighty bear has gone deep in between.

We will follow them too.
But we promise spirits when we feel a
little warmth, we will come back
to the region we know as you.

Koksijde Is Our Shamanic Name

Dear Spirits

I can hear them rustle through the wind?
As I walk, they flutter all around me.
The sea salt is touching my lips.

A sense of mystery and magic.
I talk to them.

I was made in the mountains,
but I want to be buried near this sea.

My soul wishes to connect
with you and my flesh will
finally, be broken from
earth. A bonding with thee.
Age has set in, and has taken
the best of me.
Our forefather's voices responded back:

> *The sand, the living, the life,*
> *the feel of salt water on*
> *your lips.*
> *We are all around you.*
> *Just close your eyes and*
> *feel us.*

> *Eventually, you will connect*
> *with us.*
> *This is how the human flesh*
> *merges with the skies.*

You are the living, and your
surroundings have become
a homage to thy God.

You will finally be set free.

The Big Blue Bird, Wind And
Spirits Have Talked To Me

B8- Benin

Sprits Of Africa

We were born here,
and makeup
the twelve kings of rule.
We even sold slaves
to Europe.
Rich were we.

Until ships came to
the river of death,
to collect even the
fearsome
for voyage.

In Fon dialect
We said:
"You must be mad"
Royal is the palace
we live in.

Powerful commercial empire
we have!
Pale skinned white man are
you that confused,
respect is what we demand?

The Tribal Kings Of Abomey Kingdom

Clean Spirited Soul

Oh little bird why do you not fear me?
Sit on my hand.
Connect our spirits with this land.
I am stunned by your courage.

If a handful is that strong,
I am ashamed of my own song.
Little bird why do you not fear me?

Oh, little chipmunk are you not scared of me?
Hop in my tote.
I laugh at God's holy joke.
I play with your fur made up of an auburn coat. I
am proud of your littlest thunder.

If a tiny has might,
I should continue the flight.
Little chipmunk why are you not scared of me?

Oh, box size coyote you are so close!
Are you not afraid of humans;
your enemies of materialistic growth?

Touch my leg, with affection.
I can't help but wonder if you could talk.
How some of us would then be able to
save your numbers?

If your little heart brings you this close.
I should copy your power.
Be like you, stand tall and be a great
tower.

Oh little coyote run away now,
if you stay still, you will only be bailed away
by those who are your most destructive force.

Animals always come to those with the cleanest
spirits and divine in source.

We Practice Lamaistic Buddhism

B10- Bolivia

The Landing Point, Tiwanaku!

We pray for every step
we carry our dead up.
Newly washed in God's holy
stream.

Gently rip the arms and the legs,
followed by the torso.
To create the smell of darkness.

They have started hovering
above us.
How they know our tribes
so well.

Another one,
we screech and chuckle
back to them.

Grains we put in the wounds
we just made.
We must feed these sky Gods!

Take them to the moon,
make sure they come back.

Eat the flesh.
We will collect the bones
shortly and bury them in our
sacred sites.

Tiwanaku was our earliest mausoleum,
a platform in sending off our dead.

Let these wings carry their spirits.

Our Departing Mausoleums

B11- Bosnia And Herzegovina

Mehmet Paša

Dear Sultan,

I stand alone on this bridge it's 1577.
I can feel the wind carrying the past
right through me.

The Drina river where the shamans
use to pray and wash their dead.
How violent they must have been?

I ask "how lucky I am to belong
to Ottoman territory".
This masterpiece, a modern civil
engineered pathway we just designed
will represent the future.
One of a powerful and honourable colony.

Tell me the future is bright?
There is hope for tomorrow.

A tear I quietly shed for our ancestral dead,
our animalistic believing God heads.

Sincerely,

Mehmet Pasha

*The red roses thrown today,
off this bridge is a reminder of
our continuous struggle as humans.*

*In the 21st Century with so much brilliance and
technology.*

*A remembrance and prayer of those
we lose, and continue to lose violently
each and every day.*

The Red Roses, Off The Sokolovic Bridge
in Višegrad

Running Free With The Herd

The hostile lands around Kalahari
is my home.

Many stories we tell.
These rock arts are our
cuneiform written.

Forgive us we were the first
on land, this is all we knew

Call it a constant of habitat,
some territories claimed yet barely
unchanged since the existence of time.

The limited integration which
designed a battle, between land
and hell.

Pictograms we would draw.
Songs we would sing.

Here is one for all to tell.

Chase the antelope
We run

Be chased by the lion
We run again

A sweeping Sky God
claws the back of any,
We all run!

We laugh at all of them.

Who is the real Royalty of the
land now; we tell all
these confused foreign men?

The Running Herd

Pink River Dolphin

Boto we would say,
your pinky colour just
blends in beautifully
with this tropical
landscape.

It is because of you we
feel to colour our houses
in full array.
How you talk and
play with us.

When we come to this
river basin
all we ask is a bucket
of fresh water.
An abundance that won't
bother your
way.

Pink river dolphin see
you again.

Tomorrow will be another day.

Brazil's Endangered Pink River Dolphins

B14- Brunei

Sultanate

It's the 13th century, Hindu
is our influence declined has
become our Javanese Majapahit
kingdom on our land.

The Sultan has ordered the
conversion of several
different tribes in the interior
to Islam.

They were still animists,
he said.

The caravans from the holy
lands have reached India.
And trade with them
is making us see
the light of the better
Prophet.

The glamourous mosques,
the capital will now become
our very historic

Bandar Seri Begawan.

The Sultanate's Home, Known As
The Biggest Palace In The World
Will echo the Kuran.

B15- Bulgaria

Find the spirits of the
Balkan Mountains our
shamans once use to say.

Where the birth of our indigenous people were
born.

The Essence Of The Mountains
The Romanitic Valley of Roses
Hellenistic Tomb of Kazanlak
The Murals of Spirits
The Ancient City of Nessebar

Feel Us….

God's Gift

I was born gypsy,
God's gift is my name.

A blonde amongst all
the dark haired people
I live with.

Heaven's hotel is home.
My whole life has passed here.

Amongst all the sadness,
all our people only ask
from God is as follows:

A little passion
A little money
A little clothing
A little sadness
A little love
A little dance

You have to find me, to see me.

The rich are no different, really.
This is how God tells us to be.

How our spirits should be.
These are his beliefs if he
exists somewhere.

We are his proud Gypsies.

Heaven's Hotel

A World Once Before

Was it because of age, or how species
used the land.
Before the desert and its brittle soils.
Before the slave export and its grisly
toll.

Africa was once glamourous.

The trans-Saharan gold trade
connected the ruins of Loropeni
to many other points.

The Ottomans thrived in their regions
where they were first
phonetically born.

*When trees savored the wind
in the horizon
and birds sung in the breeze.*

*When tribes decorated their Kings and
Queens, and relished them proudly in their
homes.*

*When gold and many pieces of jewelries were
made and plentiful in that zone.*

The land whispered to us its once allure.
The oracle of written bones and artefacts
now deeply grinded, broken and lifted
up by sandstorms, zone per zone.

The little green patches being chocked
by sand; the fight for survival on brittle lands.

Hides are history!
Africa how you struggle today,
what went horribly wrong?

The Particles Of Our History Forever Gone.

The Mountains

Bujumbura we dance.
Tam Tam the vibration of the
leather hide drums.

Pati Pati, the atiii
we go back and forth.

Our steps, of the movement
representing our souls.

Furious the rhythm of life,
oh how the mighty spirits calls
us all night long.

We are proud of our shamanic
mountains.
Some of our tribes call Burun.

Ut'ana the wild bird from the sky
who screams with us.

Indigenous and wild are our
dispositions.

Bujumbura we dance.
Our ancestral native scene.

Pygmoid Twa People We Are
Bujumbura We Dance
Tanganyika is our Lake

Angkor

A flash of darkness
and blindness that daunts
our earliest.

They feel, so they say:
"the blue skies are watching us".
We need to erect immediately.

Human creative genius
when no influences existed.
An interchange of values.

Of those who process ancient
cultural Buddhist traditions and hymns.

What part did Angkor Wat play
in humanities history?
Its beauty of rustic visuals and its
past.

The role of the burning in the
temple that was surrounded by
what was once holiest of water.

The eventual result became
a frontier of the highest
in early spirituality.

How an ancient world transformed itself,
into the dimensions of artistic horizons and
higher consciousness.

What is now integrated oriental art
with that of the beliefs of shamanic first.

A beauty of eerie yet daunting architecture;
and the spirits we can still feel that once
roamed its stone cold halls.

§

*A sacred site is one that is
blended into its environment.*

*Its soul is forever living;
it represents earth and humanity.*

*Once upon a time they used a
belt to seal us tight.*

Bayon Temple Of Khmer Civilization

C2- Cameroon

Waza National Park As the Sanaga river flows into the watery Wah-za Park… Deep in the jungle you will find the spirits that made humanity first start talking.	Where The Antelopes, Baboons And Lions Flourish.

C3- Canada

*The patriotic heart is our Sovereign Dominion. It is
made from the spirits of our past; those who have suffered
on the hardship of this land.*

*This applies to every citizen who has undergone
the struggle, but nowadays humanity should look
at things in a visionary way.*

It is our Natives we will proudly honour today.

*From East to West, North to South a Remembrance to the first who Crossed
They once had said
You are at Kana'da People's Standing Place*

Canada's New Skyline

Native we all are,
we really did not know.
Out came the voice of a past spirit
and now we are told.

Africa, they were born.
Centuries later the Silk Road
became their second
commute back home.

Tiptoed they eventually crossed
this treacherous Beringa strait.

Loyalist made us proud Canadians
and unique like no others before.

A mix of many other countries later,
we nestled in big grey cities,
we call this our permanent homes.

But ill started becoming our souls.
We now run to our elders
and say, how can we make
new Canada's skyline?

Using our forefather's ancient
sensory and earthly goals.

Toronto's Skyline

I Stole The Apple From The Bee

On the ground was a juicy red
apple, fallen at the base of our
family tree.

Just when I was about to
grab it, there on its other
side was a suckling bee.

Could this be the battle of the
Century?
Slowly I waved my hand
for him to fly away.
Go safely home to
your Queen.

And from my heart, I muttered:
"Sorry Mr. Bee,
but I just took this one back
for all of us to eat".

A Suckling Bee

Shaman Was My Name

Two million years ago man got confused.
He needed protection for the daily tribal wars
stemming from innate primitive behaviors of
violence and abuse.

The term called distinctions was born,
a need to separate. Centuries later, sealed became
language. What was known as the earliest vocals
or sound ranges in the ululation alert of another
clan's bait.

In era's passing, the drums and screams were
used during wars. Pastoral lands and human
habitats started territorial identity, the stems of
life had been born.

People suffered so much; socially depression hit
more than once. Switch to feudalism transformed
the role of money as a form of protective
insurance.

Caused by the bleeding heart, a mark of God's
ugly thorn.
The religious institutions became the first aid
and everything prior that once existed became a
massive illusion.

The organizations of settlement had been
established; shaman had now been officially
abolished.

The underworld then whispered to me.

Hidden in storages worldwide it is our guess there
may be some more. Many were destroyed during
the big wars but some kept them back in the day
protecting heritage and simply being brave and
bold.

Plus, your work really goes against religion. Good
luck they told me but remember the church in
many countries is still very powerful and gold.

They quietly continued. The narration of first
vocals, our shamanic past, the shame of two-
thousand years of not knowing how to bring out
their chronicles.

Followed by the real Ottoman story.

This is the very honest version of the dishonor of
our very own war-riddled ancestral past?

§

I pleaded, have mercy on humanities soul!
Make them release this immediately we are too
advance!

Are you trying to settle some type of warped
psychological and hurtful score?

Continue

These community-based institutions still need
a lot help today, let's never forget their primary
role.

To help aide the public and restore.
But gone are forced style collections, humans can
still donate to be divinely bold.

This is not the story of a diamond and a coal.

Are we not democratic? Don't turn this into a
nightmare called the academic brawl?

How about if we go slower and work globally to
bring forth.

Starting with our very own home base.
May every year on Canada's birthday,
Make it novel or old, may one country releases
something new.

A dedication to this planet's history for
being accepting of our earthly Native Jewels.

Come on world, share these records!
Our shamanic goodies of our forefathers
stored.

The drawings or written work, of their
struggles and woes.

We leave nude and not knowing,
how horribly sad is that!

The Bering Confusion

"We are livid" they quietly said. We are a multicultural country; we have encountered a problem.
Blankly they quietly looked and asked each other:

Are first clans of Earth, Asians?
How can they be if these descriptive are a form of proto- Turkic from the many regions?

Are first clans of Earth black?
How can they be if there is a standardization about them and they were found globally?
Color is predominantly climatically based?
She is right, but why didn't we think of that?

Could Natives just be Chinese now?
But they have phonetics even belonging to Europe, and Africa?

In addition, there are so many pro-types, we can't visualize these people crossing. Are we ignorant?

First clans are Turkish? That is what they are now all saying.
Canada is ruined they fumed!

We are all Turks? We are so damn confused!
We can't be link to them. The Natives are now rattled!

Who released this information?
We will by-pass her, and release this our own way they privately fumed!

§

God in this church I pray to you, injured is my soul, lost is my dominant arm, bored with tears I am.

Many days and nights at home alone, I read my hobby work to you. At home my papa teaches me Ottoman too.

Then in the middle of the night, like a lightening strike that came bolting down.
A flash I saw.

A glimpse of our unified human past. Hot water came boiling down. Helplessness was the birth of the story that developed.

Frantic to those who protect I ran? Do you not understand social development; do you wish to ruin culture? Even our Natives are not shaman but a distinct culture.

You are the highest of the light?
Release this information immediately, I yelled.

Then it all began, callous nights of house arrest, genetic tests, the violence ensued.
Call it the "Bering Strait confusion."

Continue

The hidden, this research now secretly proven.
Voices of distress is what I heard.
I am true Canadian, protect our blessed country,
and culture! From those who break the rule of
legal hand.

Horrid grief my bones are feeling. Figure out
something quick!

This was the hiccup of work, the gluing of years
of hobby work in my many nights of loneliness
that shadowed my pen.

Kanata, Ottoman Linguistic Analysis
Radicalization of language
Social Culture and Identity
The first 9 female Leads who crossed

Kanata, Ottoman Linguistic
Analysis (Unravel)
The Study Of The Radicalization of Language
Social Culture, Patenting and Identity
What are First Clans?
Landmass 1 and 2
The First 9 Female Clans Who
Crossed – Case Study

What are Hominid Phonetics?
Standardization and Relabeling
What is a Shaman!
Study of Populations
Changing DNA
Color Saturation
What is Time

Topographical Adjustments to
Landscapes
What Are Migratory Words
Impacts of Political History
Self preservation & Natural Resource Study
Social Clan Behaviors

Defining Human & Traits
The Religion of Birds
Two Million Years of Dialogues & Fire
The Fight for Africa's History
Anatolian vs. Native Connection
Who was the first Man?

Analysis of Slavery to World Wars
The conveyer belt theory etc.
Progressive Environmentalism
A Constant Of Habitat
Use Of Technology
Pictionary Descriptive

The Analysis of Land To Human
The Man Who Walked
Biblical History, rewriting text &
Our Hidden Past

Turkish Girl

*Turkish girl, who are you to tell us our own
Native history?*

Native chief don't you know,
I am an immigrant's daughter,
whose family tribe Alashan was
from the other side.

Gansu was its closest territory.
I just look different from you.

Turkish Girl
You are wrong in your descriptive
of words, we know better than you.

Native chief don't you know,
Of the nine or so female leads who crossed,
my ancient heritage is part of your heritage.
It was also destroyed
in the process of being free.

Ever heard of the Ottoman toss?
Shamanic words of first it contained,
followed by an outmaneuver and the war of
Gallipoli.

Born was I on that land.
This I acknowledge is closer to me!

Turkish Girl
You will never be one of us.
We only support our tribes, the bands
that are made up of all the First Nation's people.

Native chief, with all due respect.
Here is the difference
between you and me.
You came from the skies
and I was made in the
mountains that contained the rivers
and trees.

I am a human and this will forever now be
our connected ancestral tree.
I apologize if you look different from me.

I can assure I just understand some of your
inherited words of the first females,
that crossed the Bering sea.

This Is The Real Difference Between You and
Me!

White Negro Child

I came to Canada as an immigrant's daughter in a very poor area of east end Montreal.

My father had purchased a 10-unit apartment building from Holocaust survivors, known as the Middleman family. When at 90 years old cried when their children removed them because of their age.

The day of departing Mrs. Middleman shows us her tattoo marked frail wrists and a suitcase non touched for years, of her hat and button collection. A reminder left to us of her working in the slums of a hat factory during Nazi occupation.

This particular building was close to the oldest apartment in the area by the railways. Which interestingly held an entire building of the first Asian migrants and built not at city code but more petit in standards.

A building entirely designed at that time to these migrant's general size.

The area changed over continuously with each era bringing in new immigrants from a diversity of backgrounds. By the time we had settled an influx of West Indies had immigrated and had taken smaller size apartments in the area.

The weight of managing a building alone took a horrid toll on my dad who now became an absentee parent. My mother on the other hand completely new even in communication became isolated and developed mental despair.

Corn braided was the hair of my adopted mother. The inside of her palms unlike others was a beautiful light ebony black representing one part of her interesting Amerindian background.

A trait left only to a very few indigenous remaining in her parish, in the island of Barbados. Technically the few left in the entire West Indies.

Child she would say for a white girl you have thick curly blonde hair; you must have black in you.
Growing up with them, I would yell back don't you dare call me white. Confused horribly at my identity mixed in with them for years.

Her own daughter and I had made a pact to be blood sisters for life. Our community of island people was comprised of a school that had a black female principal and black teachers. An attempt by Canada to make comfortable its influx of island immigrants.

The Black Community Centre that we would go to housed the oldest Centre in Canada to improve life after slavery was abolished. Established by Jewish and black female women, trail blazers they were named, for attempting to push progress.

Continue

Today as we look at the beauty and variety of the multicultural families across North America.

A new bond of integration and tolerance is forming.

Merged with the development of my own historical timeline, and the research presented to University of Toronto to demonstrate the irregularities of defining humans in the light of academia of past.

We can justly mark this as monumental defeat towards evolving. Called humanities push in civil and human rights in the 21st Century.

I can honestly say I am very proud, I was raised as a white negro child today...

C10- Canada, Quebec

C'est La Vie

Non, rien de rien,
non, je ne regrette rien!
Ni le bien, qu'on m'a fait
Ni le mal; tout ca m'est bien égal.

Pour nous
C'est toujour c'est la vie
Aujourd'hui, hier et à l'avenir
nous ne regrette rien!

We have Quebecois French....
In Vieux Montreal

The Blue And Green Hues Of Earth

Our early humans first saw only two colors as divine, they then asked:

What has the skies given to us in terms of defining humans as superior beings?

What has these blue hues given?

The blues represent universe, it simply taught us tolerance.

The act of loving all the imperfections, cultural variant, physical and topographical designed traits the heavens have created for them here on earth.

§

What has these green hues given then?
The land simply taught us where our souls and history germinated from.

That the dirt on the ground has to be felt, touched, and made respected.

Our single source or connection to protecting the planet is part of all our lineage.

The Mergence Of Sky
And Land

C12- Cape Verde

The Isles Off Africa

Christopher Columbus said,
"What beauty are these islands
off the shores of Africa.

Our stop is temporary, the pillories
all across the island
upsets my soul too much.

Plus, this area is secure the new
world on the other hand allows
us to explore a lot
more for our country."

Christopher Columbus's Visual Of Slaves
In Historic Cape Verde Pillories.

Chari River

They have come. Be careful child.
Call it the devil in disguise. Deep into the
marshlands they went; slavery decimated its
original indigenous.

But by the hopeless river,
take a second and study
the channeling flow of breeze.

And its gushing swell.
That once carried water
to the many parts of its Gaoga
empire.

Animals, the French had yelled.
They wear vibrant feathers
and run half naked amongst the
low plateau of savannah.

They do look graceful though, we must
acknowledge. Blended in spirits, when they kill
not a single animal runs.

Our guns strike many down.
Empty we will make their land.

In one hundred years' other tribes
will move in.
We will continue slavery till no end.

Flowing Through The Wind,
Were Once Our Riverine People.

The Shamanic Prayer

Sing praise
Sing praise

To the terrapins
linked to the skies.

The moon glistening and
translucent in nature.

Vibrant is the mist surrounding our Shan.
Smokey with the dust they spew,
lifting our spirits.
Sing praise
Sing praise

To this food given, protect us.
Now we we do this for you,
oh Josh-hua.

We dance, the shamanic way
Chosmak, our wild native dance
around the bonfire we twirl.

Circular in format.

Hide our faces with earth
materials blessed from
the clouds that hover.
Sing praise
Sing praise

May our souls be heard.

The first tamgas of earliest life,
the skies have given us.
We dance for you.

Our Prayers For The Skies

The Stan's Of Central Asia

Kazak
Krygz
Other tribes within Russia
Tajik
Turkmen
Uzbek

We are what is called in Farsi the
residing area, of our standing people.

The variety of indigenous known as
our tribal name plus our place of
stand (stan).

Our tribes are all different.
Our dialects identify one another.
Centuries prior we would continuously
battle each other.

Today we just tell the world we don't need
to, diplomacy is our rule.

Our borders were created to now separate each
other.

Our flags tell the world the differences
of one another.

The Different Indigenous
People Of Turkic Countries

C16- Chad, Republic Of

Quilted Tapestry

Your prehistoric Neolithic sites
scattered throughout.
A quilt woven of
over 100 different languages
and dialects.

A rich world not known.
Of opulent literature representing
the creations of first life.
Millions of years of verbal history
illustrated through picturesque rock art.

Kingdom of Kanem.

Ignorant man be for not understanding
the tribes of Sara, Tangule and Buduma
to name a few of the many.

Your black-blue skin of beauty
that once had traversed.

Had originally linked your tribes
to many making up territory from
the equator line to the base of the
Mediterranean Sea.

Your quilt centuries long
represent one of our most ancient
start of humanity.

The Negroid Tribesman
Cave Dwellers
Was Your Oldest First
Recorded Ancestry!

The Black Mummy

We are the ancient ancestry to the
Picunche people;
we have just invaded another tribe.

The women are ours.
The men and children we kill.

The children we feel somewhat
remorse.
So we collectively pick
a few and put pelican skin
on their faces.

As our youth prepare them for
the afterworld.

We eat some of the body parts,
urinate on them
so they don't return to kill our own.

We cut our own hair and pick the adolescence in
the tribe who
have seen 10 winters to put it
on these new mummies.

We are attempting to desecrate
our enemies' ancestry.

This is called our ritual of manhood,
where our youth have to stuff them
with earth, and cover the empty
body cavities with ash paste.

They have now become men and
will learn to hunt some more.

Once the mummification process
has finished we will dance, and eat their food.
We have to be sure their spirits will not
be an omen to us.

This is called our spiritual prance.

Has One Slipped and Returned?
The Essence Of The 5,000-Year-Old Black
Mummy

C18- China

Peking Man

Peking Man known as cave person,
can you hide anymore?
You walk half up, right and down,
oscillating left to right.

You eat raw meat.
Yet you fear like the many
other animals from before.

Cave person
When did you become human
is not the key?
Barefoot and torn were all
your feet.

You started with a few words,
and the utilization of
tools in your bag of hide.

God put his hand on your
shoulders one day.
Made you permanently
stand upright.
He went on and directed angels
from the heavens above.

Help them educate
the divine way,
the holy book will be sent
and made in gold from the skies.

Cave person something
magical is happening now.

We can reveal your history
accurately and not be bound
by the historic reason's
hidden by God.

Cave Person How Did You Stand Fully Upright?

C19- China

Dark Fairy Mountains

Our altar to heaven
were the mountains.
The magnificent seven
were they tip by tip.

They were called
Peri-shan.
To eat means the holy
shamanic seven.
One more ate, after eight.

Ustra did they bring.
Known as the tips of present
life sorrow a culture of utmost
devastation.

Our shamans,
brought them food.
Their elaborate ceremonies
of prayer and sacrifice.
The sprits of destruction
became our,

"Dark Fairy Mountains".

China's Seven Mountainous Points

C20- China

He (ké.key) is the name of the flowing river.

Hé

C21- China

Your Majesty,

Our people have so
much honour.
We too are Royal.
Ornamented we brand
them in red.

We were the first real
humans, refined was our style.
Why do you hide
thee?

We had pyramids
before others,
we had written
before others.

We also migrated
to Africa,
thousands of years
prior and integrated.

We produced gun powder,
astronomy, nautical and macaroni
noodles to the world.

Our battles were fierce.
Mongoloid labelled, were
we back then.
That others claimed all of
these historically.

Ignorant be not!

Your own people, your heritage.
Part of Europe's ancestry,
is also linked to us.

Why do you hide thee?

By Little Emperor,
In Big Man's Shoes

Blue Eyes

In southern Turkey
elders would say,
blondes were our first.
Blues we were meant to stay.

Overtime our clans grew.
Discrimination we did not.
What is a human, we knew
back then.
Interestingly from Egypt, to Algeria
all got thrown in our evolutionary pot.

A few humiliations and defeats,
our trails became too wide.
Lively-hood in pace,
growth was still our pride.

Transitions from one point
to a next,
conquering became our
trade.

Kiev became our second
home.
Never once did we betray.
Time went by, the depth of
intermix became our bay.

Elders in southern Turkey now say,
hazel eyes were our second,
beautiful light browns we were
meant to stay.

The Evolution
Of Changing People….

C23- Colombia/ & Armenia

By The Railway

On the railway to Popayan,
we arrive at an ancient kingdom of 1889
called Armenia.

There the name resemblance echoes.

A prayer is told:

Greater is he than that which is in you,
out of suffering the emergence of
strongest souls behold.

Be still and let the lord judge
the wrongs of those that once
were uncontrolled.

The guidance and gift of
higher force,
we thank your power
O'Lord.
Amen

Blessed Be Our Existence!

The Essence Of Vanilla

The rain sinks so
deeply into the lava,
that the porous rocks
of Grande Comore turns
the water to brackish.

Yet through the hard
conditions of land the
vanilla oils
for export are still
provided to the world.

Mount Kartala,
before the haven of pirates or
man became permanent.
Before James Lancaster ships arrived
in 1591.

Do you remember?
The tropical climate,
the hand tied twig floats to cross.

The bare and injured feet of the many that hid on
the island for centuries.
The beauty of land, its birds and lemurs.

The influx of African mainlanders of
mixed diversity which became the start
of our permanents.

A story of life, way before Jumhuriyat
became us in 17th Century.
Our people a mix race making up
Africans, Arabs, Indonesians
and Iranians.

Who like our ancestry, just enjoyed
the wind and the salty air.

§

Pirate we may be, but our ship anchored,
full of men.

Thou can not be afraid of anything.
Including dark hiccupping mountains.

Congo's Genocide

For each era that has come and
gone, violence has consumed us.
Middle Africa.
Not 1, 2, 3 or 4, more, like 5
million or more.

All painfully brought to earth,
with love and care.
Evil became the rage of the lifeless
bodies who were mutilated and sent
back. The catalyst of what is horrific
warfare.

The shred of women's pain;
hours of bonding between
womb and life,
so ignorantly disregarded.

Not a single remembrance globally
for future children to shed a tear.
Lower than our animal instinct,
the value of no human worth.

The truth is the dynamics of pressurized
soils became the tragedy of what
was to be unearthed.

Pain beyond belief.
The heaven's now proclaimed:

*Always give a hand
to those in need.
Communicate for civility and you
will forever find relief.*

*Put seeds of bloom,
as remembrance for the
decease.
Make this tragedy of souls,
never ever re-bleed.*

Keep the memory of these deaths alive,
our conscious always has to be
vigilant.

The cherishment of being human, a concept
to be made doctrine by heaven's earthly laws
and distancing of animal dissident.

The Flowers Swaying In The Breeze.

Teke, The Minority Is This Tribe

The visible is obscure
Ku Ku Ku …
We mimic the one's in the sky.
We the ancient Kouyou people!
Tribes with feathers
we were not liked.

The Italian-born French explorer
Pierre Savorgnan de Brazza
in 1875 made a treaty with
our other people the Teke.
That made their territory under
French protection.

Utu was our earliest sung,
by the river near the Bembe
watershed.
Elastic was our bonfire dance
of life.
We now became a different
game of delight.

Ku Ku Ku…
We were never liked.

Ku, ku, ku
We Once Had Called Upon
The Ones In The Skies

Tropical Nights

The indigenous desire in me,
they said we have none but
I ignore.

I feel that I want you,
that I need you.
Sorry for melting in your arms.
You are my life and spirit,
you are in my mind.

Every time I see you I feel
beautiful things.
Desire, oh desire carry my
lighted torch.

Give me the chance to be on
your side,
if you leave I will never
forget you, please come back to me.

You give me the strength
to continue.

Tropical flowers make up
your scent,
the silk of your hair,
the touch of your skin.

Its desire, oh desire.
Continuing burning in me like a flame.

The Passion Filled Tropical Nights

Pygmy Hippopotamus

Shaman youth
we are together for a long
time in this tree.

When I screamed for you
to climb,
I pray to the ones flying,
you followed me.

You see that thing in the
water, it is watching us.
These ones are smaller in size.
This does not matter.

When you come close to
the bank and lay down
on the ground to drink.

Once you see those small ears flop
back and forth.
Run like a lion was chasing
you and forget any of your pride.

Run Shaman Youth, Run
Our Forefathers Paid The Heavy Price!

Wild Horse

Wild horse are you tamable;
find the other one hundred
that has abandoned you?
Roam do you do,
so iconic in nature.

The biggest colt of them all.
Near Livno the plains of heaven,
your fields way beyond yonder.
Rugged you climb Cincar,
your spirit wild and free.

Wild horse,
will you submit to us?
Our farmlands are way too many acres;
hands we would need to help feed?

The souls of those who once
try to grasp you still can be
felt in the nightly breeze.

Run wild and blend into your
picturesque scenery of
our background homeland.

The terrain of Duman, makes up
the smoky grey streams,
and rugged stones under
your galloping hooves.

Make us watch your precise beauty.

Oh heavens, there had to have
been a creator!
Your exquisiteness in the wild is
beyond any artistic belief.

Coldblooded Horses, Croatia

Oh How I Love The Cuban People

Their beautiful brown skin, and mix of Spanish-Afro style beats.
Their humbleness to God, and being human.
The safest of all the islands.

Oh how I love the Cuban people.
Their old American landscapes and cars dates back to the 60's.
They would sing me their version of love to the skies above.

Guantana mera

I am just a truthful man from the land of the many palm trees. Before I die I want to share the written love from my soul.

My poems are soft green.
My poems are also flaming crimson.

My verses are like a wounded fawn seeking refuge in a forest.

Guantana mera

My words are spoken sincerely,
and rings in with hope for tomorrow.
I speak of life and its promise,
I know its joys and its sorrows.

The streams of the mountains
please me more than the seas.

Guantana mera

I always say I choose the poor as my people and share their dreams and their troubles.

"The prayers of God are what we all look for."

Our Indigenous Devotion
We Join In For
Their Love Of The Skies

C31- Cyprus

Run My Loved Ones!

The war is here, villages
they are plundering and burning.

Our people are so human.
They have been casted an evil
spell.

Mother and her three young children,
have run far from their homes.

Where the father awaits
to divert the enemy.
You may be able to save yourselves he whispers to
her.
Don't look back he says.

Dear skies,
I am praying to you so deeply,
Listen carefully a man wounded so horribly
with this world's agony.

My faith has finished here.
Protect my family he glares.

Beads of prayers in one hand, the dull kitchen
knife awkwardly in another.
The half night so bright, innocently he awaits.

A sniper pierces right through
his body.

Split second of memories
quickly flash by.
Years of love making,
holding hands,
his own childhood
and his children.

The land of vineyards and grapes hanging.

His other half on the hill top
watching the body being flung
around by the many darkness of foreign,
quietly wails.

In the distance hearing the chimes of Ayia
Sotira. The promise if something goes wrong gets
fulfilled.

Humanities Tears Of Remembrance

Christ's Halo

The poor begged for his life, with no avail, they
started to pray:
> *Tar o, lay low*
> *Tar o, lay low*
They quietly cried.

Don't eat God's chosen one, on this old rickety
wood cross.
> *Ku ku ku*

The punishers called on the skies with anger as
they set him up.
Take
> *Al – amin'a, inan-na*
> *Al – amin'a, inan-na*

They screamed in retribution for
her to come down.

A small child rapidly darted and gave others the
message. Those around him were very poor yet
they ran and sacrificed a deathly thin animal,
close-by.

Hopefully the ones in the sky will stay busy.
While we bring him down, after dark. They
whispered.
> *Tar oh please- lay low*
> *please- lay low*
May these terrors leave.

Dark clouds over us.
We begged the skies for mercy
on our Chosen's life.
Up goes another one, and another.

Focus on our lead they say,
his purity and halo blessed.
We quickly kiss his feet.
His fresh blood marks our face.

Please fight for your life.
Cries, the animal sacrifice doesn't work.

The smell of blood,
quickly attracts the many spirits of
Tar, in the skies.

Suffer we also do Ana, to save him.

They hear, we will never change our
many terrapins.

Watch them, they told the Marytr ones.
"Eat You Alive!"
> The Start Of Transitions Has Begun

*Vatikan when I wrote this was my sensory wrong
or offensive, I had asked, that I be locked like
an animal? This single poem is presently part of
blacklisted book called Rewriting the Religions.
I write fictional again!*

— D —

The Cultural Touch

The journey across Scandinavia, one of the strongest holds. Its Gothic cities and landmark heritages, couldn't digest what was being told. I had to be clever and real fast, if I was not I would definitely not last.

Denmark is the center of civility and law, is what they barked! It has been this way for years; this is the only way we know how.

We have many things completely distinct to us, including the oldest welfare system and benefits if you must.

In addition, might we say, beyond human we are a Christian God's perfect development.

Call it our etiquette of civil sentiment, our service to our people.
Our upper class.

But there is another side to this I presented. Don't be surprised now that Denmark has relented.

I said don't get confused with the picturesque marks of earth a lot of us all see. Like tectonic plates stacked one on top of another, the first words of life, are the emergence of our very own history. The dark to light, like a spectrum of colours. These were simply blended in with the animal howls of our first others.

Disorderly is humanities first dialogues in what is call our earliest jubilee. Jutland became an example, a form of early singing in the breeze.

Remember from Europe to China back then took only two years for the migration to flee. Denmark understand what it is to evolve and it will make you see; why dialogues became one of our ugliest political decrees.

The theme is now shamanic; designated once became your clans. An attempt to convince them further, with legal right. Follow green for it is the path of our aura of lights.

Your indigenous past represents a different type of flight. It is one part of how humanity will last, something horribly missing from our historical past.

The illustration has become human interconnectedness our road today in advancing. This is how humans will win, with zero might
The Development Of Culture

The Nissum Fjord

The glaciers cut deep this particular Fjord. Formed from glaciations millions of years old. Its 100,000-year-old first settlements. Whispers to us the spirits, of what was once told.

Each year that had gone, missed something, from a story so old. Here is of how simple the land developed our first tasks. For this, we will now commemorate our shamanic past.

Our ancestry has become such a great honour. A calendar is one example of the visuals of what the land had to offer.

At the start of equinox each year, the waters levels let us know that winter had elapsed. And spring will allow us to bare. Back then we knew no better than what our land the fjord, told.

They became our only measuring point the marks of our ancestors, and their existence to live practically blindfold.

Sanskrit and Hebrew were linguistically no different in the development of words from other zones.
It is the age of Europe's historical habitat that is the question of the birth of this linguistic loan.

The start of descriptive visuals if I must say, possibly thousands of years old began developing in the oddest of ways.

Ni-san is Hebrew, while Ni-ssum on the other hand was Europe's first in the same inverted way.

But it was Asia's Gods, their spirits, making holy their water called Tan-ni. The irony of it being from around Hindustan, thousands of miles away.

Makes this story slowly starts to unfold.
Which regional phonetic was really first, we will never truly know?
Nissum Fjord, the land, the visual and the story that became unfold.

§

Dear Copen-Hagen University,
Come see the sorcerer's crystallized glass ball.
Was your ancestry not from the vast territories around Caucasus regions of Asia?

Don't let the swarms of black ravens following them, rip their flesh again in the after life.

White shaman the waves of the North Seas are not calm. Man is man, animal is animal. The past healer's spirits have whispered to us.

Sincerely,
The Heavens

D3- Djibouti, Republic Of

The Market In Djibouti

The Afar or Danakil people
have seen the Portuguese, Italian,
French and other African traders.

The oldest caravan routes were linked
to their Abyssinian plateau.
Where you would find the Centre of
Djibouti city life.

There in the markets, centuries ago the following
items were sold:

*Food, daggers, knives, necklaces of amber, wooden
objects, root-dyed handmade outfits, silk and
silver jewelry.*

Today when we go to the market you will find
the following:

*Food, daggers, plastics, knives, necklaces of amber,
wooden objects, chemically-dyed outfits, silk and
silver jewelry.*

The locals say our daggers
may be the same,
but *this world* has changed
so much.
Maybe our old traditions
were the better ways.

D4- Dominica, Commonwealth Of

The Boiling Lake

This person is a witch,
an omen from the sky Gods!
The Carib's once said.

Throw her into the boiling lake.
Watch her spirits melt
and never come back.

Smell the sulfur and flesh mix.
When the bones are left.

The dances of death we will do.

The Real Thermal Springs,
Called Boiling Lake

1844 War Of Independence

Please bless us and split
our island in two from
the French speaking dark-
skinned Afrikana tribes that
conglomerate to the West
of our island.

We are not like them, at all!
Our people are of mixed blood.
Hispaniola and Caribs, are
to name a few.
But we even have German Jews in all of
this brew.
We are way too different
culturally.

The split means we are finally protected
in our perspective territories.

We can now celebrate this grace of Victory.

Our own designed cultural costumes, folk arts,
dancing and music- Made us proud Dominicans
to show our difference from them!

E1- Ecuador

Almost Human

Man said we came
from ape.
Women said we are possibly
still ape!

Ecuador became the footsteps
of this researcher's holiest place.

Through dense jungle, Darwin's
path she wanted to follow.
In search of defining what is
human this time.

Forested indigenous,
barefoot you walk.
Wild is your look,
with eye-make up
so stalked.

Tell me if you have seen human?

Yes, we have:
  They are here protecting
  the forests.
  Praying to the skies,
  And living in peace with their surroundings,
  around them.

Forested indigenous, have you ever heard of
Darwinism from possibly another researcher that
may have travelled along? But more importantly
of how man was derived? No we have not can
you explain he smiled:

  They are here swallowing up everything,
  they are on earth even extinguishing forests.
  Believing we just showed up with no belief from
  the skies.
  They are destroying all their surroundings.

Forested indigenous can you please pray for us.
Your humanist soul is what we need right now!

In Search Of Human, Indigenous Man!

The Spirit Of Tutankhamen

The Valley of Tombs.
A king's reign, vaulted in,
opens so slowly.
Hieroglyphs now give us
such a story.

The son of Merit-R⬚,
a king by some
known as the Pharaoh of the Exodus.
Glorified, the blessed soul of Africa's
Tan was he. Amen!
He was just one of the many.

A prior disposition to represent all of
the black charcoaled out-lined eyes,
of our shamanic past. Amen!

We call on you holy spirits in the sky.
We worship the heavens,
the many priests who had
aided his essence in the process.

Deity after deity,
we had prayed to the heavens. Amen!
The tower of pyramids,
were made to honor the many who had
passed by.

Amen!

Wings had once adorned our sphinx,
humanities confusion removed them
satanically.

Little is known on our real history.

In the essence of life today we
are attempting to do such a recovery.
The substitution from Amen to Aten
occurred; may he finally rest.
To Aten!

The very slow conversion from Atentism,
its solar disk to Egypt's monotheistic beliefs.
A cultural development and a look at our
own progress, at its very best.

§

The "Bird from the East" told the story about
Egypt and their sprits as being one of the world's
oldest continuous settlements.

The Spirit Of Tutan

The Warrior Known As Musa

Prior to the Red Sea parting;
before any exodus;
or the onforan of Canaan's name even
being part of the lively Neolithic
coastal, existence period.

Their also existed Moses
but his shamanic name was Mu'sa.
From ancient Persia, he came blaringly
defiant to survive.

Migratory were his clans,
with very large stallions.
His team was strong as hell.
They destroyed everything in their paths.

Centuries later, during the luster of the
Pharaohs in Egypt, holding an infant out
of the Nile's water. A voice whispered,
your survival, call it a decree predetermined
by God:

Child, you will be adopted and
geared as our own son, my priest
will bless you. You too are a Musa.
A word to mouth story of a warrior's
past historical strengths.
His legend trailed through
the centuries of life,
when no real written existed."

But it was God that made the most remarkable
spell, when it came to Prophet Moses. He blessed
earth for what is betterment. The reason behind
what God
said to Moses:

"Selected, I have deemed you now as having
divine origins. For the ethical and moral
teachings, of the ancestries of your clans".
Remember what is human and
these sacred scrolls.

Your people are Chosen humans,
designed with no flaws.
Perfect in human intention.
You were design specifically from heaven.
Even before you were born.

Just fill your prophecy!
A transposition has taken place
and forget your shamanic divination,
for a new light has been born".

The Transition To Monotheism
And Prophet Moses

Spectrum Of Light

We were born from a single
bacterium that replicated
and carried the
photosensitise of light.

Migratory and crawler
became the living
as the tectonics of earth
changed their part.

Some formations became
spectacular
no different than art.

Corals, pinks, azure
and sangria reds
are just some of the
colors that gave way.

It designed all the
creatures of earth,
in the most sheerest
of delight.

When we look at colors
Let's understand all
the hues.

For all our vibrant forests
are merely a by product
of copied light.

We are thankful El Salvador
for the reforestation introduce
to increase our colorful lives.

The Colours Of Life

E5- Equatorial Guinea

The Fang Chief Said:

If you and a fool dance,
you will win.

If you and a fool have
an argument, he will win.

If you and a fool make love,
You will both win.

As a chief, speak only to those
who are above you.

Traditional Worship
Is Still Really African.

E6- Eritrea

The Admiration Of Aksumite Empire

We were independent until we
fell under Ottoman rule.

We taught them what our
forefathers use to say.

That compassion was developed
from three words.
To see, feel and act.

What our earliest saw;
What they felt deep in their souls;
And their reactions to their outcomes.

Anyone acting immorally we would
let them bleed.

We are still part of this legacy.

Ak the symbol of spirits that are
flowing, called the white of death.

Aksum Region,
With Its Westward Flowing Rivers.

The Transformation of Tallinn

Bipedal barely, our first humans
were screeching throughout Europe.
By the shore of Tallinn, they dragged
the bodies by the feet
to feed their sky Gods.

Epochs of slow light and
distorted time.
A flourishing town, gradually
developed into the Hanseatic
League.

Estonia's became a trading city.
With medieval times churches
and its castle that housed its
crusading knights.

Nowadays a remarkable urban
fabric with European style
precise geometrical structural
forms.

Winding streets and fine
public burgher buildings.
Restored is St. Nicholas' Church.

This is the very slow transformation
of just one historic European city.

Heritage at its finest best.

Tallinn

Kingdom Of Kush

Earlier than Selassie,
Ethiopian born,
I ask you.

"Why do you adorn yourself,
with those colours,
of green, yellow and red"?

Child do you not know?
"These are part of our shamanic
rituals of past".

Red is the blood that our forefather's bled.
Yellow was the moon and sun
we prayed to.

And green was the religion of earth
before any man settled.

Earlier than the Solomon Dynasty,
we are the historical first civilizations
of Africa.

I understand this, but why then
do you follow the revolution
of stars?

Child do you not know?
"These are our shamanic
beliefs of the past".

The stars guide us to the
Kanat that flies.
Their beaks carry up,
our ancestry to the hungry Gods.

And our Kingdom of Kush is where
our territories began, way
before any man settled.

The Flag of Ethiopia

The Moon Dance

Underneath the moon
we dance.
In complete darkness,
the sole light that exists.

The multitude of the lunar
faces, we study.
Our palms reach the skies.
We ask for what is in between
the moon and earth Mez-ayah,
we scream.

Our symbol for illumination,
and some warmth.

Many Gods hear our voices.
Protect us, we say.
From the curse of darkness that
doesn't fetch our ancestry back.

With the faint shimmer
of hope, all we ask from you is,
take our dance and mourning,
and bring these spirits back.

    From The Skies To The Torah

Two Wild Horses

Put two wild horses
in an enclosure,
they will madly kick
around and even try to bite.

Watch their struggle,
in a web called the
unknown fury of life.

Even if one is bigger
and the smaller is getting
injured in the end the
horses know their destiny.

Its masters have locked them
together in a small holding area.
They gradually over time
get use to living with this
dominance of might.

This is called the analogy
of social behavior.
Helpless these two
horses are now unified in a rut.
Both understand they are destitute
and jailed in.

To the powers of a master's vision
of humbling the beauty of wildlife.

Humans are no different
and are also sealed
into earth's walls.
They too feel helpless
and locked in.

But this time the skies are
our master, they are watching over us.
Humbling continuously the beauty of
their wildlife.

Helpless early humans then
developed the many "Laws of Life."

Do you now,
understand how ethics and rules were born?
The power of humans to be civil in
earth's walls of life.

The Wild Horses Of Eurasia

The Birth Of Satan

Ruler of the dark,
the one evil that can control earth.
How did you come to be?

Your wings filled with might,
your mouth hovers over our dead.
Did we do you wrong that we mourn
today?

All we ask from you was the
noblest pleasures of earth be ours.
Contentment, we wish to pursue,
without the darkness that comes to us.

Oh spirits, talk to us.
Salvage us from this dark ruler of Tan.

    Şey-"Tan"
        Say-"Tan"

The evolution of "Satan" has began.

God's Lack Of Authority,
The Revelation Of
The Black Mass,
In the Valley of Doom,

By Satan

The Group Of White Knights

White men adorned,
were our Vikings.
With shamanic head gear,
That converted to steel and
heavy armor.

Never once did we see
anything so fierce.
The family of druids were
their leads.
Around the henge,
into the uncharted.

Little clothes in the winter,
fearless in nature.
Wild in behavior became our
white ones with metal gear.

White Knights follow the rare white raven
to the seven megalithic monuments,
and have your nobles pray to the heavens.

The Private Race Of Man

When all men on earth once
came from different sources.
Animal we must still have been
for not seeing the light of
the work presented.

In a dark room locked in I am.
The role has flipped,
as a researcher, I
actually study them.

A secret, my sensory
now picks ups.
Of a fierce battle in Geneva
that has began.

Of what was first race,
their dialogues and who was
actually first man.

Like blood in shark infested waters.
I watch social mock of each other.

The highlight of distinction now broke them
into a massive flutter.

I raised my hand and
quietly said: When you accept and face humanity
all of you will be able to advance today.

None of these arguments are important, if
you can just define to me what is
"A Human?"

That landmass one was two million years of a
blended fusion that made our earliest
handful of shamans.

To that of a gradual saturated DNA
mix, human adaptations and a lot of
academic past confusions.

The uniqueness of God's creation was
centuries of saturating his species.

The colours, styles and shapes of earth were
made because of the design of topography of
their many lands and the bodies of waters.

Define Human?

— F —

<table>
<tr><td>F1- Fiji</td><td>F2- Fiji</td></tr>
</table>

Paradise Cove

Well my friend,
Our people like to eat, sleep, drink
and be in love…

Paradise is all we need!

Kula Eco- Park

We constantly sing in the mist of the night, but
one thing I must say to you.

If there was only one moon, I still would not
share this beauty with you.

F3- Finland

The Boy And His Lantern

Hei, my name is Hans Christian
he whispered.
I am so wet and it is cold outside,
please can you let me in?

It is spring and it still feels midwinter.

Child which district are you from?
The man asks?

We live at the base of Haltaitunuri.
The war did so much damage,
and I have another 10km to go
before dawn.

The man's fire-light was dim,
here take this he said.
It's a small glass of wine and a roasted
apple, please just stay warm.

Hans continued, I have landmarked
the pine trees, this is the way I
reroute back home.

The peat bogs I keep slipping into,
the wax I carry is enough to bring
me home.

When the rain stops,
I will make my long journey back.
I really need to get home.

§

The Dark Timber Is My Soul.
The Finnish Elk's Footsteps
Helps Me Get Home.
The Lantern In The Forest

Fontainebleau

Sitting nude
in the small vibrantly
clear blue creek.

Near a tap cracked opened
by the pressurized
mountain's vein.
My black hair dangles.

I am life!
I touch my breast.
A uterus in floating water.

My leather hand made
shoes hung on a low
tree limb.

Place in the sun
to dry the scent
embedded on hide.
A smell of earth mixed
with human sweat.

Hoping the impact of man,
doesn't rip open my soul.

I ask the spirits
please but please
protect me.

From the surroundings
I live in and our earth's
dangerous tolls.

The Uterus In The Floating Water

The Breaking Of Human Distinction

How dare you they barked,
we are not African or coming
from there!
What are you trying to say?

I said humbly

    You may be right, or
    you may be wrong.
    Do the test called
    the nipple size
    and it will solve the
    problem of your day.

Don't get offended with the
colors of first,
we all came from ape.
This is not a curse.

You need to change
how you think.
And our missing ancestral
link.

The moving DNA that once
roamed, our spirits of past
life to that, of what is a human
chromosome!

Let's forget everything for a
minute I say.

The focus is social betterment
and this should be humanities
new way....

Defining A Hominid Trait

Nuit Noir

Windings roads, cobble stone floors.
Tiny flowers each window still
carries high.

Hold a glass to the Eiffel tower;
Chardonnay, Pinot and Bordeaux.
Are the wines in aged display
in each corner store.

The life of a Parisian.
Historic and rich, full of lively core.
An opulent cultural mixed
with old and new.
Artistic all displays are, in imminent form.

But have a look at their language
and let's not be in the dark,
anymore.

England had all the fun!
With hat, bat, cat and mat.
But it didn't finish there.
Many more existed all in
the simplest nursery-rhyme form.

The French language is perfection
in its altered state.
We can analyze these dialogues
further, can't you see the precision
of this grammatical state!

They brought out Bescherelle and
thousands of verbs, all in enlighten form
with complex structural schematics.

To tell the world we were and still are
the highest academically, a brilliant mode.
The reason is simple. English is way older
if we attempt to put it chronologically.

Hittite started the base of phonetics from the
very start of their cuneiform tablets found
underneath.

France at the time was nowhere near, this
developmental build. The language known
as romance, came way later. A design
constructed very organized and clear.

Contemporary Francien!

F7- France, Normandy

The Battle Beyond D-DAY

I walked into the historic hall entrance
of the University of Toronto.
There on a plaque is a reminder,
of the boys no older than twenty
sent to war.

Cold brass had become tarnished,
forgotten with the stains
of tears over the years it was hung.
A list way long.
They fought for our freedom.
How fortunate we are;
as I attempt to see if I can dust one corner.

Thousands died on the beach in the
first five minutes.
Some yelled for their mothers.
The bullets were made in Germanized,
newly designed auto-format mould.

Pierce through several times
their thinned out bodies.
Etched became their memories
on Omaha beach that day.

No different than their earliest
ancestor's battles for survival.
The blood soaked sands became
just another defeat, another reminder.

Today through understanding
and human consciousness,
a long journey our road has become.

One towards advancements.
We pray for their souls.

We proudly shine their plaque on the
wall to remind us that as humans we are
still in a fierce battle.

An enchanted gold gate,
gardens of birds and flowers.
Living we want to place back.
May their innocence or suffering
be turned into a bed of roses.

Called "The Giving Back Life To Those
Who Died Violently."

F8- French Guiana

Majority of our people are mulatto,
like they love to say.

But our blacks speak Taki Taki,
and refuse to be address to downplay.

The Tribes That Once Had Said
     "We Don't Like The Mulatto Way"

— G —

A Spoon Made From Food

We have some interesting dishes.
Our original inhabitants were in majority
Pygmy who consumed very little meat and
were masters of life within their equatorial
rain forests.

Our regions nowadays make up forty
different territories and languages.

They will eat a variety of food.
Antelope jerky, salted fish, fried bats
and roasted caterpillars to name a few.

However, even since Neolithic times our
early morning meals remain the same across
the shorelines of the Okano river.

They will collect edibles and crush them with
heavy stones. These early inhabitants have
given these ideas to most of the people
across Gabon, and even other tribes around
west Africa.

They moved from one region to another
completely biodegradable in form.
The Pygmy's would once say, be clean
don't use your hands.

If you want a spoon for your

breakfast you will have to mold it from
the pressed grains we have provided
and then use this edible serve to eat.
The water with heated grains comes
from the sparkling blue rivers.

Fu Fu it is called our popular meal
with no utensils, just a lot of fun when we
eat.

Our tribes Carry Only One Woven Basket,
It Is Our Entire Home.

G2- Gambia

By Gambia's River	
When these European explorers first arrived in the 14th century they came to our very large kingdoms. We kindly showed them our woodcarvings, batik cloth printing, designed weaving, gold and silver jewelry making. Something interesting happened like it was their land the Portuguese sold trading rights to the British and all of a sudden Fort James was built here.	The Batik Method Of Dyeing Clothes

G3- Georgia

Why Are The God's Crying	
Why are the skies releasing tears, the darkness pounders light. Fear runs through our shivering bodies. Why are the God's crying? During Paleolithic times we hid in what was once called the departing caves. In the mountains we gradually transformed these death dwellings into Vardzia, our permanent home. It was our only form of security from invaders who had avoided the caves of death and "the Gods" in case they sent their omen wings after us. Mortified in thought we still prayed for life. The fear that another one, will not come back? Why are the God's crying? We wait till the skies stop.	Ziya, The Candle Light Of Death

Bird In The Wind

One by one they filled
Germany's ghettos.
All selectively sent,
another side to Schindler's list,
one that never really has unfolded.

Papers were scattered on my desk.
Night after night,
the dawning inclination that
there was more of Ottoman
then what was historically told.

The only way to understand them,
was to envision their strategic view.
To understand the mind
of what is called a radical pursue.

The war began,
symbolism they needed.
Something indigenous
taken from the land.

The running bird in the
wind now became their new
ugly force in command.

Machinery after machinery,
what a push for control.

Not a bullet was needed!
Advance and leave them
nude for five minutes in the
coldest of the cold.

Underground secretive treaties,
Russia would have had to have
quietly opened doors.
What was Hitler really looking for,
only a select few will know.

Claiming Back The Indigenous Symbol

G5- Germany

Aachen Cathedral

The prophecy from the skies said
"Be aware!"
From its inception the screams of
past can be heard.

The torment and torture to convert.
The painful transition that had to have
existed on earth.

Don't be idle for the earth will
continue to be a Gaia.
The skies had said.

This became humanities enlightenment
the relics of the clans that pushed God's
word.

The Souls Leaving Mother Earth

Saint Ursula

The unlucky Saint Ursula was the lead of the
11,000 virgins reputedly martyred at Cologne,
now in Germany.

This was done by the Huns, during the 4th-
century nomadic invasion of southeastern
Europe.

The ancient basilica wrote: We are respecting,
of those who have died as holy martyrs,
therefore, we erect this church.

The Struggle Of Women

Once upon a time,
we were supreme.

Out came foreign.
Flipped on us the
power of our own
being.
The struggle of women,
now broke us.

Once upon a time:
    We would choose our men.
    We would choose when.
    We would control the family.

Violence on land made us
secondary.
Never envy us, all men.
Our strengths are delicately
woven in with softness.

Our struggles are pain
beyond belief.
Humbled has become us!
Our spirits are chained as
our core sits on its course.

Torn are our souls, ripped inside
with the life we bring.

All we ask from God
is simply one thing.
If we return make our
lives more bearable so
we can eat.

The Tears Of A Woman

Earth Became My Zoo

Help I am in a massive cage.
Earth has become a holding cell,
called my zoo.

God I curse you every living day.
Why place me here?
The animals I deal with in this way.

Torment my spirit behind these bars.
Gods eyes are my only vision,
I ignore those who pass by.

No different than a caged
animal but this time human.
Another place has the better of
spirits, the collection of wounded.

Doctors don't understand me.
The numerous types of dopamine
I need, to prevent me from
going crazy.

Depress is my spirit my world
is so uneasy.
I don't vocalize.
Feel me, I internally scream,
in this cage I now wish to die.

In the end I know as a human
we can go out and flutter.

Then I think, an attempt to
heal my soul.
What about those in our
surrounding; really stuck in a
cage of steel.

Our animals; one of past karma
now merely part of our human
dominated lives?

Maybe to better ourselves
the least we can do
is increase consideration.

Recognize the show.
And make our own worlds,
more unpolluted with love and
compassion.

Sensory And Compassion

A Secret

Deep in the dark corners of military bases
everywhere. Academia gives
intelligence the statistics of our truthful
plight.

We are this short on water,
barrels of oil have dropped.
Tundra's baselines are royally being
cut. Please can you help maintain us to
prevent further ecological disasters.

The light continues:
    Furthermore, how do we tell women
    the grisly truth?

    When love hits the feminine,
    many feel it's the baby
    that makes the man
    fully glued.
    1,2,3, and 5..

    The role of religion, domination or the
    sadness behind this immense lack of
    control.
    How do we verbally communicate
    this heavy reproductive toll?

Today as women, we hold hands and stand in
front of you so humbly. Words of wisdom,
empowerment and prayers for other starting
so innocently.

We have a secret, the female voices of reason
say, we have the strength that can be
modernized in the best of ways.
The light of earth's betterment that must be
portrayed. The rule of thumb is to stop doing
fierceness men and let women vocally be.

To the bearing females we guide you always:

    The lesson of womb is simple you see.
    Regardless of who the love is.
    Ladies remember, two buns and
    your done philosophy.
    Never forgetting that ancestry is really
    a 25-year responsibility.

This will design a better place for you and for
me.
It will also make our world of intelligence not
be covertly managing and have faith in
humanity.

            The Value Of Human Life

I Grip Your Head So Tight

Love is beautiful but
today is my way.
I mark your back and
grip your head with my
strong arms.

Furiously I make love to you,
the testosterone in me that
was way over due.
The skies don't judge us
for even the animals
do the same.

We were all made equal
from the soils that germinated
this truss.

What others view in modern
times as a divine shame.
Just enjoy this game.

Our Love

Whose Monkey Is The Better Monkey?

One monkey, two monkey, three.
Which one now became me?
Dr. Seuss you were the God,
I now take over from thee.

Once upon a time we had many
different monkeys.
Colors, their traits, even some fur
came blatantly through.

So much enlightenment we lack,
education we now fight back.

The philosophical question that
reigns over us is, which monkey
is the better monkey of you?

Snowy were the ones from China.
Furry knuckles were the ones from
Africa. Round eye chimpanzee mixed in,
entered Europe and Anatolia.

Are all these monkeys confusing you;
because we can even throw in a tail
or two, in all of this migrational stew.

Compete we did for centuries;
outburst of violence and fights.
Different races we got confused and
encroached the many lands;

using it by not understanding this glue.
The confusion of what made up an enemy's
bite.

If we think about it,
Adam and Eve were not really
Biblical, if we see the academics behind
what is really right.

Cross reference don't you dare.
Little did humanity know we
were designed from a monkey's traits,
in one massive animalistic delight.

The Evolve Series Is Coming Soon!

G11- Greece

The Greek Goddess

Real woman you were, with hips so wide.
North Africa's whites were some
of your oldest lineage.
Anatolia made your ancestral people's
resting place, a blend of all three continents.

Your curly long blonde hair,
olive skin became the exotica of a
phenotype, designed by the symbolism
of white and blue.

The thickness in your breast,
so succulent with no disguise.
Your beauty caused the Trojan
war and the series of omen injected
vengeance, of other women's cries.

Helena you were in spirit,
an infamy of true female,
and the desire of numerous
men.

An evolved Venus.
The earliest beginnings
of what became today
the Queen's of all the heavens.

A representation of all leads,
started on this planet
with a womb like you.

The essence of the first desiring
female Goddess, that others
simply pursued.

Helena, The Greek Goddess

G12- Greece

Konyaliyim

A division of the ancient Greek people, even found in Hittite records.

For over a thousand years, our family heritage was from Ionia.

We are the people of Konya, we proudly once said I am Iconyaliyim, Konyaliyim.

THE SPIRTUAL, ONCE LANDING ZONE

G13- Greece

The Skatan

Skatan we hate,
not to be mean.
We have trouble,
feeding our might,
of 50,000 strong.

Skatan no more,
we leave your
violent manners.

The rules of God,
are now encoded
in our soul.

Civilized we are,
democracy and philosophy
we bring to light.
Far from your ways,
of primitive delight.

Bitter turns to mockery
call it centuries of ill.

The beating heart
their skatan
turns to skata,
and that is our will.

Dance Wild Around A Bonfire
We Do No More,
Instead Carry Our Torched Light.

A Mix of Three, We Became Thee

A petite island, 200 Km,
in the Mediterranean Sea.
Is our Crete.
Maritime Minoan is its history.
Its people are a mix of three,
from one end to the next.

When confused Anatolians would say:
"From one end of Crete, to the other end of
Turkey" (Ya Hanyaya, ya Konyaya).
They strongly still professed!
But let's not forget Africa, in all of this bless.

Many things have come and gone.
Rich became their story.
The historic divisions of four became their
small regional territory.

Khania, Rethimnon, Iraklion and Lasithi.

Where Khania is now pronounced Hania,
but Konya is still Konya, gone today are the
variations and mockeries.

Modified may be their language,
cultural heritage is their story.

Ancient Egypt and Mesopotamian
trading was the center, once upon
a time of their historic glory.

But mixed of three are their people.
Crete from one point to the next.

Minoan Goddess

The Fight For Arctic

Our land was so quiet,
ships would even
have a hard time
passing through.

Our people, of Inuit and Eskimo
extraction; lived off whale blubber,
and raw fish.
Sunlight either too much
or too little.
Would determine the light
for kilometers away.

Then one day,
a few too many ships
started passing through.
Man did so much
damage abroad.

They began searching here,
hoping to resolve all
their woes.

They started disturbing
the underground.
Cracking the ocean floor.
What on earth were
they looking for?

Fix your own surroundings,
we politely told.

We represent tribes of
the Greenlandic people
and want to remain clean.

Not in between your battles and
environmental wars.

John Davis Strait

G16- Grenada

New Grandada

I took my friend Ada
to Grenada,
The local said *"are*
you grand like our island of 1498?"
A corny joke came blaring through.

She said "African I am",
Proud is my heritage.
But never forget
so are you.

The local laughed.
Sugar and spice,
and everything nice,
is our island.
Cod and bakes are
our happy food.

Smells cinnamon, clove and nutmeg,
every single day of the year.
All part of our ethnic food.

Vibrant in colors are our people.
Tropical now has
become our flavor.

Like everyone else who left
the mother land.
Just a different time, and one of
an unethical plan.
A different culture is what we
grew into.

My great grand papa was even
born here, this is all we knew.
I am a proud Grenadian hope I am
not sounding rude.

More simply put,
does Africa have any of these plus
some punch-a-rum, too?

The Wind's Borrow

G17- Guam

Chukchi Nomads Of Guam

We are the Chukchi; part of the Paleo-Asiatic
nomads.

Our penis's have roamed Siberia, Guam and the
coast off British Columbia.

The numerous loanwords in our dialogues
links us together with Tungus, Turkic, and
Eskimo People.

I Love God

A transformed angel with wings and might.
Wrap me now, and hold me real tight.

Like an eruption, I begged for life
I can't breathe.
My love for him is that deep.
Many dark clouds later,
I discover,
all the benefits that I will now reap.

I love my God,
a hand he had loan.
Lifted my spirits,
those that were torn.

Mayan Indian I am;
a soul so pristine.
Brought me now the happy
spirits to my home.

Visions today I now incorporate
like a sorry song.
I dictate a section of Miguel Angel Asturias
to him,

I woe to him, Lord,
he who doesn't exhaust his supply,
And, on returning, tells you:
"Like an empty satchel
is my broken heart."

When you look at dark and nothing
makes way.
When a void fills your world.
And sadness tears your heart away.

Just love your God
inhale his power,
miracles will happen
that is all I have to say.

§

Our forefathers would say when the heavens
open the sky they created a transformed
angel. Take oh dear heavens.

Indian, Then Was Taught The Bible.

Guinea Fowl

Good morning my friend,
how many eggs did you produce
for us?

We really need to eat!
For centuries you are
definitely God's blessing
to humans.

Stay close to home the
big cats, snakes and civets
may also want to eat.
Our reason is, he who steals
an egg will steal more.

§

To the Baga people, its 900_{AD}, we the Susu
people have now come into your territory and
have pushed you aside.

Its 1300_{AD}, The Portuguese came and push the
Susu to the side.
In the 1700_{AD}, Islam came and started a holy
war.
In the 1900_{AD}, the French came and made
Guinea an overseas territory.

Recently IMF came and that was the end of it all.

The Fowl!

Traditional African Religion

Our heritage is based on oral stories
rather than scriptural.
We chant and dance.
We believe in a supreme
creator.

We have many traditions like the
practice of blood sacrifices, omen
spirits, and veneration of ancestors.

We use mask magic, and medicinal herbs
as part of our ancient customs.
Deep in our hearts most of us ignore
what foreigners injected into us.

Our four ethnic groups are the Balante,
Fulani, Mandyako and Malinke people.
Whom maybe all different,
in their every day interchanges of
African culture.

But majority still have ancient customs
we call real traditional African religion.
Our faith determines the spirits,
we try to restore.

*Children find the passion in the lion
and it will give you power,
unlike before.*

Our Animist Beliefs

Sleep Peacefully Mama

I am a Proud Guyanese!
Proud Afro-Guyanese,
to say the least.

Indentured slaves were the other half of the people that were brought. My great grandmamma, rest in peace, was even Amerindian.

A blood wrapped infant she was when she was immediately separated at birth. Little is known of her earliest, other than recalling the word of mouth stories and a few words of what the land tells us today.

Our countries name Guiana, came from the Indians they would claim. "Land of Water", this is how it is recorded in Guyana's history books but I believe it actual originates from early slavery.

An anchorage stop that brought in our first black slaves.
Disembarking them to an area of their records, being their affiliation in France. A harbor named Guyenne. Possibly synonymous with their land of water, a port found near a region called Aquitaine. That the Dutch gradually picked up.

Called the first visuals of French sailor's note-taking records and what they quickly labelled as ownership. Part of their, then historic Nouvelle France, empire schematic growth.

History so convoluted, as I try to gather very little pieces of me through her, our proud Indian heritage history.

My notes in my journal continues.
A remembrance my Amerindian grandmamma would do, to even her late second mother, a negro female nicknamed Dada.

A female who gave, her own breast, when her own biological child was removed. To prevent unwanted conception during rape; a woman who fed her continuously till she reached the age of four.

The small handful of memories left to her would have been a loving hard-faced women closest to her as a mother figure. Who passed away when she had barely turned six.

The many tales told to her at night in the crowded chattel sheds. Goosebumps as she would try to recount recollections of her own great indigenous history through the narrated, stories.

Continue

Her bright black-eyes closed, she could only dream.

Wonderful feelings would whiz into her, sitting amongst the wild flowers in her vivid thoughts. The blow horn of shell to call one region to the next. The smell of raw meat on fire. The hide of animal as a cushion for the floor they would sleep on.

The stories would continue, Ana'h our great forefathers called upon mother earth as the highest of all the females on this land.

Their words of wisdom are what you should always heed.
Wondering since my own childhood about all the females on my mother's side I did not know.
I keep these narrated stories as memoir for you.
Young child this is not much but it is all I have.

Some days how I wish, I would wail. Just to touch their black silky hair and feel their skin.
Mother and son we stand by this shore,
as we look at the skies we pray to you,
may you find peace in your spirits
as we call out to all of you.

Kneel And Pray We Will Now Both Do.

— H —

H1- Haiti

Red Voodoo

Painted faces,
eyes rolled back.
Straw dresses.
Combined with chants,
and animal sacrifices;
we do all this to
transform reality.

Our sacrificial red
is our favourite colour.
The one that stirs iron
and fire.

We dance and ask the
spirits to bring us
back the ones that
are with our flyers.

Voodoo dolls with pins
inserted in, first
made from straw.

We do these rituals to omen
those who hurt all of you.

H2- Haiti

The fighters said this land is mountainous, we
can hide. These mountains carries our wounded
blood.

From Africa their spirits echoed:
Behind the mountain there may actually be
another mountain.

Proverb

Haiti is the world's first black republic.

The Secret Lines

Cuneiform tablets, buried deep in soil.
Everything burnt and flatten on top of
the mountain's heavy toll.

An archaeologist said in 1934,
these written marks are Indo European
words on Turkish soil!
He read slowly, the lines on the clay scrolls.

Nu Ninda-an ez-za wah a-tar-ma.

I felt a correction of work had to be made.
Studying, for fun, the earliest dialogues of
our forefather's today.

They were a panel of professors sitting
gracefully. May I add, my own version,
a twist of life's funny irony.
Can I present the sad of many centuries.

The hidden, their chi still in the breeze?
Understand these ancient and very old written
scrolls. There is more to the nail
chip by hand and baked clay, the
marks found on Anatolian soil.

These are slow transitions from one
language to the next.
The dying of linguistics and the
changeover of our phonetic co-share
words from our shamanic best.

Some came from the east; others came
from the west! Hundreds of thousands
of years' prior sounds were naturally
incorporated in the heart of what was
once the Hittite Empire.

The marks above similar to Ephesus' entrance
should now read:
Bu Ninda-an ez-za' wah a-kar-ma.

The kings said upon entry,
follow the path of holy water.
Our point is the one that is
closest to God.

Anatolia known as one of the oldest crest,
these words made up an ancient world's earliest
cleanse.

Today these regions should be known as the
temporary home of English languages first
dialogue structures.

Cuneiform Tablets

H4- Hebrus River, Bulgaria

Beyond The River Evros

Akkad's our tribes are.
From the Mediterranean to mid Iraq
are our territories.
The streams, are our pathways
we followed.

Damaged papuk, our feet worn.
We wash each dead,
in one tributary
and drink from the other.

The mountain's flow continuously
washes our sin.

Following the animal trails,
to nourish our tired souls.

Looking for our only means of
survival, the meandering Ak,
of streams and pathways.

Our only true judgment,
is our needs.
The hills for our spirts,
what the land provides
and the life we call holy waters.

The Flow Of The Maritsa River

Captain Henry Morgan

Goodbye Elizabeth. Don't wait! Loving you brought passion to my soul but understand the only loyalty I can profess is to my King and my country.
You are a beautiful woman but my job is horrendous. Our many fleets get emerged underwater, we have even lost a few at sea.

The waves are as high as mountains. The gigantic surfs make the strongest of our men who can even lift our six feet anchors feebly ill.
Find another passion you only deserve the best and wipe your tears. Our battles with the Spaniards in Panama was an encounter that nearly cost me my life. There is a good chance I may not return.

This time Las Barbaras awaits us, we have to carry live cargo and our men get very ill with their diseases on board. It is so bad when we disembark the locals have to give us lime to prevent hurling and have even nicknamed us limey's for looking that green.

I will give you some advice Elizabeth it is the secret of all Seamen, never ever put your heart and love in a Captain again, especially ones that carries the stripes that represent the "*Kingdom of Lions*".

Weeks abroad, the solitude of the seas.

We are almost on shore, now men be very careful! These local women are beautiful. Their long strait black hair, almond piercing eyes and strong legs will entice you. Do not commit mutiny, you must remain dedicated and loyal to your country.

You may unchain the deceased that is left on broad and clean the feces two days from now. Until then our live cargo gets released first. Have some compassion, they are sitting in urination and blood for weeks and are deathly sick.

Our job is to protect England's interest first.

§

Captain "Sir" Henry Morgan 1674
You, Sir Henry Morgan have been so dedicated to your country, privateer they call you. We beg to differ. Your act of courage especially against the Spanish made our country bow are heads in respect and honor.
I, King Charles, have now appointed you as a hero to the British Empire and Monarchy.
May your title always represent the highest civility we will give to the world.

Counting Sheep

We own this land,
safe we thought ourselves
in the mountains.
These barbarians have ransacked
everything!

They took grain,
set the 3 village homes on fire.

The worst is they scared all our
sheep. 1,2,3,4 and 19 all jumped off
the cliff in Kekes.

No compassion these animals had,
can you imagine our wound when
they only stole three.

Now we have no food to eat.
How we pounded on the icy soil
and cried.

All we do nowadays is suffer with
famine and at night count sheep to
let the cold winter months pass us by.

Prior to the Mongols these cliffs were called the roaming Tekes hills.

The Dolls Of Iceland

Humans once looked for the rare ice flower in the snow, a message was sent to the heavens.

Everyone's vision of beauty
is different.
Each culture that comes and
goes has their own ideal
that represents inner soul.

But some were designed by God's
perfection rarer than others,
this you should know.
Increasing the mathematics
of demand in attractiveness
and the bold.

The Dolls of Iceland

Made of glass and snow.
The skies added the bleu,
a rarity so deep it belongs
with a crown in a chateau.

In the end perfection is what
is bestowed.
The Dolls of Iceland

Were given to us by the heavens.
To match the crystal hues of the

sparkled flakes on the icy land,
to where they were born.

Thou art indeed, Your Lord

12- India

Ram Is My Kar

Ram is my Kar,

whose head sits on the platter.
The nightly dances of headdress,
each manhood dances with.

The wind that wakes up,
the scent of those that
are in need.

Ritual after ritual,
blood drips.

Scorned are the heavens
in the sacrifice, they call
kur-ban.

Yet hopeful are those,
that pounders over
the meat provided.

Ram is my Kar
that is feasted upon.

Decorated Were The Ones On The Stands: Called shamanic Kur Ban.

I3- India

The Revolution

We see the light and
social ethics were born.
Eco-warriors is the Shiva
of fierce spirit in us.
We are sick of everything
suppression is no more.

The study of human social
behaviors, came out.
This time using history
and what went wrong.

A path of green warfare
Social injustice
Connecting DNA
Merged are these concepts together.
Angry to high hell,
we all are.

Revolution of the womb,
survival it has now become!

The Revolution, The Official Name For Survival

I4- India

Sanskrit

Kind and gentle words makes everyone happy,
take this papyrus and try to write the earliest
phonetics to give to humanity.

Bha, Li, Mu, Ni, Ri, and Za

The Missing Link,
The Forever Gone Papyrus Papers

I5- India

Ignore Monogamy

We are indigenous wild and free!
We love the forces of life.
Aryans first invaded us
3,500 years ago.

We told them and our scholars
the same, ignore monogamy we want to
make love to everybody.

A Catalogue Of Desires,
The Temple of Love India

I6- India

Sun Temple Konârak

Shaman we are,
we lift our palms to the sun.
We ask of you,
find us relief from the destructive
forces around this land?

We carry this tiny body.
A common occurrence
of illness which took his life,
from the land.

Unlike others,
he was born to earth badly deformed.
We knew he would not last
and was an evil from those
who screech at night in the forests.

His soul will not be fed to the flying
ones in the skies.
We will simply chant and dance.
That the demons, like the bewitched
women who made him don't come by.

We will rip both mother and son
apart and give this omen to the woods.

Scavengers will consume both of them
and we pray, others like them will never
reincarnate back into our lives.

Konârak you represent ancestry and
the one in our skies.

We have begun to question supreme.

The Living

Ever see the magic inside
a rain forest shimmer?
Colour laden are
its vapour filled mist.
So delicate is its land.

A rainbow god would have
had to have merged land
and sky.
Done with love and
his hard labour.

Burnt orange are its orangutans,
baby blue are its fish.
But there is something
you should know.
Lethally deadly, that should not
be missed.

Clay are its dead soils,
delicate cover it needs.
Pangea once attached the land
before the split of all the
turbulent seas.

Lift the trees and its suckers,
desert will be its
new name.

Know the value of compost,
Sahara was once lush and the same.

A membrane so dark and
delicate, earth needs to
survive.

Protect it with vengeance called
God's grandeur designs.

The spirits of past living and
their ancient residue that still
moisten the skies.

*The Spirit, Mother Earth Hands Holding Water
Underneath*

Assassin

We wait for the monstrous
enemy on the hill top.
Fall bait to us please,
we have no mercy.

Sold was our secrets
to the kingdom.
Our messengers did they
kill.
Blood wars did ours become.

Come in, come in.
Show a blank face.
Feed them hashish,
then kill them slow.

Europe will one day
make this famous,
and transform hashshashin,
to assassin.

A word to remember this
fierce enemy's blow.

The Caves, The Hideout of Zagros Mountains

The Three Prayers And One Sacrifice of Elam

The elder came in the tent.
You have to give him to us!
No, the women wail.
It has been 20 moons,
she is not going to recover.

She has lost a lot of blood.
The elder man snatches
the infant.

The five brothers follow him
to base of the Elam plains.
They put the male infant on an
Altar and commence
sacrificial rituals of Anshan.

The dances of manhood begins.
Ones to make clan men strong.
The others to remove omen.

Dear sky Gods, we are giving
you back to him,
for the lost of Yacoub's concubine.

Just when the dances hit night, a child comes running over. The mother has awoken, please stop. She is wailing and will poison herself if the infant is not brought back.

The men think the women are attempting to outsmart them. Into the animal hide tent they all burst into.

Please elder, I kiss your hands, a voice faintly whispers by the candle glimmer. The mountains sent my spirits back may I hold my firstborn, please. The men stunned handed her the child.

They brought the full fed newborn back to Elam plain, the next day. On the altar they gently placed him.
They kept his tiny body wrapped; in the same white linen, as a reminder of how unlucky he may have been. Called the white linen of death.

Ezra, is now your name. A reminder of the mountain's heaviest toll on us.
A small mark we will do on your forehead with a knife. You will never have to do the ritual of manhood at the passing of 14 different seasons.

They lifted the child high above their heads, we are grateful Elam for not bringing us darkness and for granting us our blessings. We thank you for not taking one more of our dead.

The History of Persia

I10- Iraq

Feeding The Sun God

Married to my first born daughter,
we know no better.
Then to go to the hilltop
where she will lead.

A place magnificent to see,
Mayan my beautiful queen
how I love you.

May your blood dripping
be the chastity, to feed the Sun God.
May your body coil around me
to keep us warm.

Your hair of youth,
will wrap both of us.
Married to my first born daughter,
we know no better.

How I will enjoy you.

Human Start of Life and Incest

Ottoman Head Quarters

Sultan, we will set up three critical
points.
Vienna we went all the way up to
and was given the hardest front.

Yet we still couldn't access their gates.
Mosul, Konya, and Basra are now our
new headquarters.
To control the westward coming Mongol
attacks.

North Africa was always our
territories.
Istanbul we acquired in 1453.
We still want Europe, Sultan what
should we do now?

Gather all their foreign women caught,
throw them in my Harem.
Kaya Kadin will calm all of them
down.

Let shame all their tribes.
If they do not bend to us,
we will weaken them by
showing their ancestry
what could have been.

The first decease child in the Harem we will send to them. Send the messanger, put the Sultan's Stamp on it.

Tribal We Are

Barbarians they say we are,
they do not understand tribal
warfare and what is hunger?

We come into Al Amarah's region.
It is the first crossroad of
another tribal clan.

Our battles are fierce, we take.
We desecrate their tribal name.

Our secrets are simple.
What is the first thing, we look for,
even before we eat.
Are their women we wish to
plunder.

Our manhood will protect them
to carry our lineage.

Self preservation is our marry!

*Men we kill; henna, soil and root decorated tribal
women we plunder.*

Uri

I see the full moon but await
till everyone is asleep.
I sneak out; my tender breast makes me
the youngest of the entire
family tree.
In the dark I hear my name
softly, Uri are you there?
My lover a man more than
two times my age.

Love at first sight, he grabbed me violently
during water collection.
I fell for him.
*You know I will die a million
deaths for you, I touch his
hardened cheeks.*

The mountains have to forgive us for
the love we make.
Next season they want to marry me.
He stares blankly at me while he
pulls out of me.

We are a different tribe, Uri and they refused the
bride price we offered to pay.
Don't sacrifice yourself, my love
to the Gods, he says.

Marry him.
Cut the womb gently inside
with chopping chisels.

Glue it with a mix of lemon, bark sap and molded
sugar.

They will never know,
that your price was lower.
Then poison him slowly.

As a short lived widow,
they may find you omen
and wish to forgo you.
Beg for life.

Cry you never had love for him.
You wish to live.
Then we will continue our
love.

Uri we have no where we can go.
The mountains, the moonlight in the
darkness is our only sacred home.

Castle On Inishmore

Once upon a time the Celtics settled in Anatolia.
A regular transit path was this warmer land. They
could not take a dwelling or two.

If we do not leave, violence will be the death of
us. It will continually ensue.

A few thousand years later, they found their own
lands and blended many times violently with the
migratory indigenous of the region. Where they
then settled and made their permanent homes.

The low lands were very cold, but fish was
abundant. "We can change some of these rock
type Henges," they said to be an even stronger
and safer fort.
Visiting Ireland, you should see some of the:
Old turf homes blended into
Ireland's landscapes;
cultures exhibits; and
its monuments so great.

But if you want a spiritual link,
I mean one that connects humanities' soul.
Look for the words their forefather's carried.
It reflects the footsteps of our earliest, the start
of faith and the pain with it, that was once so
abhorred.

Take a side trip to the Aran islands. There
perched on an edge, enter Innishmore, you
will find the magic of this 200ft cliff ahead.

Still very indigenous, the ruins they would feed
the hungry birds, called Dun Aen'gus.
Part of their Gods, which was an angelic first
move of humans' early past .

Walk slow and just imagine 8,000 years ago,
the struggle of coping to understand
transitions. The tears of letting go.

That cliff they fed the skies their families;
a most strikingly unimaginable path.
Stay on its tip, if you may and
be like them as you feel the gust.

The view from its rampart, their aura and the
sea.
Now imagine, how they let go of their
ancestors, the centuries of corpses and the
clasp of a deathly breeze.

Spirituality means feeling their ancient shamanic
tease. Inishmore cliff you represent their legacy a
different type of heritage for humanity to now see.

Adam or .....

In a region of antiquity, centuries away,
many traversed and was one of the most
divine in countless ways.

Hava, Awa meant skies,
but so did the origins of Eve!
Found everywhere lets further study
this female she.

Paired together,
Adham and Eve you were
born Hebrew biblically.
Did anyone else ever wonder if
there was actually more to thee?

Israelites are the Chosen,
it is said in the Bible.
The only ones first link to higher written
devotedly.

Part of their sacred scrolls of Ivri,
pronounced Eve-rih is where
the story start.

Now I sit and wonder?
A theology of written seen on a black stone,
a window of past life perceived in highlighted
writings in my head.

Ivri has to be the first spirits of womb.
Another clue will forever be my secret of how I
decoded this, a study for hours in my head.

Rih became her energy that used the
serpent to tempt his soul.
A male form that was wrongly fed.

Even back then the source of life,
were the female Venus's in lead.
The mother of all of earth,
I concluded is our historical missing key.

If we look at this religiously
the story merged together
transformed itself to the "Myth
of Origin" as a biblical she.
A distancing from any animal,
as a life in a uterus brought the first
human he.

A local word Ivrim further starts to bring
the possession to these sacred text.

A ownership of life, one that meant
Holy, devoted to the ones that profusely bled.

<u>Continue</u>

Ivris' scrolls today started the birth of Eve.

One day it became encoded
in all the prophecies from above.

The reason Christ's acknowledge the
chosen people well and gradually
transformed, our Eve, the written
account of Genesis, to the guiding of
what is a human and that of a single deity.

Humans evolved when a full conscious
was actually born, so <u>for centuries</u> when no
written existed
the liturgy of divine text is the story
that unfolds.

Adam and ….

*The origins of God in revealing human
then became the story of Adam and Eve…*

116- Israel

Ahu'di

Ahu'di we look at the sky,
our feathers in different array.
Painted faces we howl to the moon.
Don't use your might or your claws,
omit us from any type of pain.

Ahu'di we rip skin,
a painful ritual to become men.
Our finger nails still carry
the flesh of manhood.
To show you our strengths.

Ahu'di we ask,
"why do you devour our dead"?
Eat our food we kill for you
instead.

Masada the hilltop of sacred feast.
We ask you to bring them back.
Ahu'di became your mark,
the power of your fame.

*Yahudi is Anatolian people's reference to very
early indigenous bird believing Jews. It still means
Jews today. Reference 5,000BC and prior.*

The Elder Of Safad

Elder why do you sit by this
Synagogue for hours?
He would say,
I find great peace secluded
in here.

This is the oldest synagogue in the region.
The Sephardic Ari
and represent healing for me.
It connects me back to God,
our cemetery of ancestry is
a remembrance
just two minutes away.
A closeness I really need.

Elder you still have a family spend time
with them.
My protection of family is not needed.
My children are all grown and
my life is God now, with my other half gone.

The reading of the Torah makes
me strong.

This is where I wish to die.
An odd pleasure I feel as the
breeze hits my soul.
Let my homage and respect to
that of the skies
be what is the best for me,
the keeping of spirits, as a whole.

Our Elder By Safad

The White Lion Of Golan Heights

Once sacred was your home,
able to tackle down a large
elephant alone.

The other beasts did not torment you
on that soil that also use
to freely roamed.

How green was the land you
once had
called your own.

The Golan mountains use to say:

> *O sanctuary, a place you have made home.*
> *We will do a homage to a King,*
> *in these Royal lands.*

> *You make the valley's weep with the*
> *fierceness you bestow.*
> *Arise and go forth let people feel*
> *your spirit.*

White lion stood sacred and alone.
Mighty was your kingdom,
the essence of what was now
transformed.

The Sighting The White Lion
Of Golan Heights

Yehudi

Conquest was our might,
holy is our land.
Yehudi are the ones
we collected globally.

Our land was protected.
We roam, free to be.
Now by divine's touch,
chosen became our spirits.

From pointed grunts to
looking at the moon.
To Ivri the birth of Hebrew.

Hanna was our first,
Star of David was our eldest.
Our forefathers followed the thin
animal trails.

God's will for Canaan,
Divine's resolve and
perfect aim.
Our ten hands still touch the
skies.

Blessed were we,
merged together.
Holiest sites we pray.

To others we say: "*We are the chosen people
belonging to the promise land,*

Eretz Tzion v' Yerushaliyim"

The Seven Day War

Annex was this war,
called the six-day war.
To grow our holiest land.

God blessed,
its people with a call.
That there were many
other regions to commemorate.
To say they were the forgotten
ones.

Made in Ahri'da,
her birth year was also 1967.
One day more, than the six-day
war and seven should then
become their luckiest.

A reminder call and whisper that
said..
  "Do not forget, the
  ones who's spirits hid in the mountains.
  The many regions whose forefathers,
  fully developed language.
  They also roamed.

  The synagogues in these district,
  their other first settlements.
  Cultural artefacts left behind
  equally important as the holy lands".

A prayer's call is needed.
For the spirits of the forgotten.
They innocently said to the mighty
rulers at that time.

We are proud people;
with their local shamanic verbiages
of past they once had said
we all are Yerushaliyiz.

A private message to Israel from the author
regarding their Ottoman history and the conflict
of what is defined as a cultural heritage.

Dedicated to Our Ottoman Jews

Marco Polo

Its 1271 and we are in Indian territory.
Venetia all the way to the east.
I have education and a good knowledge
of their Koman dialects.

In the freshness of the night,
they point and say it quick.

Hindi is some sacred landing site,
all in the north.

It doesn't matter, we still cut across.
All their territories,
Yunnan, Kafiristan and Cathay
to name a few.

Travel we do from one
point to the next.

Koman is their dialects,
and I am the first European to
reach all the way through.

Marco Polo Travelling, In a Tatar Outfit

Roma's Mark

Polygamy,
Bestiality,
Art,
Cathedrals,
Heels and whips!

Roma's ancient and
trendy culture.
Really hip.

Pasta,
Grape vineyards,
Leaning towers,
Aqueducts
and
Historical fleets of ships.

These are the social
marks of a culture,
today in full fashionable tips.

Designed by centuries
of artistic genius
and fashionable
illumination.

Roma's ancient and
trendy culture.
Really hip.

Human and Goat, Sexual Indecency.

— J —

The same bird that will carry news, will be the same bird that will fly back.	Jamaican Tody (Todus Todus) is our bird.

J2- Jamaica

Bob Marley Identity is what is designed when people had no media and became individuality of one of a kind. A tiny island in the Caribbean Sea. For four hundred years became the way, of its highest in spiritual blue peaks. A genre of music that was called the consciousness to the extreme. From a descent of slave. Lyrics of a true soldier that gave way to our global heritage gift.	Heard even in the smallest of pubs in Tokyo. May he rest in peace. A person who became an example of expression of individuality beyond belief. Bob Marley

J3- Japan

Our ancient rituals of death. The place our forefathers souls are washed for the heavens. *Osh' aka*	Osaka Wan

J4- Japan

Shintoism My power is the most potent of all weapons. It is the analytical capacity to know divine spirits. These are from the teachings of our earliest nature worships. Even before the many prayers of celestial were created. We never forget the divine, goodness given to us by God. Where misfortune is averted and sickness is healed. We only blame ourselves for the lack of teachings. We are the ethical content who will now fulfill our obligations to our ancestors. In believing!	Japanese Shinto Structures, Starting 6th Century

J5- Jordan

Dry River Valley Sandstone and granite are its mountainous surroundings of heights of over 1,700m. Its narrow gorges, fissures of carved natural arches and 25,000 rock carvings. Once upon a time there was a flowing interaction with our natural environment. Wadi Rum was the place of cover, that even the seven pillars of wisdom were written about. Its shamanic name was once known as the cool flowing river valley.	Part of Rift Valley

— K —

Dark Wings, Black Nights

Lethal is your span.
You have become our symbol of
warfare.
Chants do we do to you,
in the tundra of the night.

Beet soaked flags with charcoal,
adorn were our first drawn in wings.
Power we ask from you.
Our blow banners change,
with each of the directions
when we followed you.

Only wings do we carve
in our armours and coats.
An emblem of hidden past;
a struggle of our silent foes.

Dark wings, black nights,
over thousands of years.

Became our heritage symbol.
Many of our forefather's
remembrance of battles
and tears.

Our Kazak Emblem

K2- Kenya

Hours Spent Studying Fingers And Sky

Man saw the skies,
and elaborated our devil has wings.
The thousands of years of transformation
to angel.
Where did this come from?
Half bird, half human.

He lingers over us like a dark shade,
they once had said.
The noises he makes.

Kik became his first name,
Uyu became the permanent
sleep he acclaimed.

Don't wake,
how they begged.

Kik uyu *sleep please*
Kik uyu *sleep please*
They quietly said.

We mimic you only to be fierce in battle.
The violence in other territories rage.
So many of us die.
How you devour our many dead?

Fear us, to others they howled,
like we fear the darkness that comes
from in the sky.

Kik uyu *sleep please*
Kik uyu *sleep please*

Only bring omen to the ones we desire.

Kikuyu Tribe, Africa

K3- Kiribati

Magical Phoenix

When the sun goes down in
the Pacific Ocean.
The coral atolls shine,
and the waters underneath
all come to life.

Luminous the moon hits
the surface,
pristine are the life beneath
that never sleeps.

In the dark is when our Phoenix
comes out to eat.

The Moon in Tarawa

K4- Kosovo

The Ova Of Birds

We stand around a fire
in the region known as
black birds, and pray hard.
Mighty one, hear our souls.
We have seen so much
violence.

The "Ova of Birds" represents our spirit
that makes us stand tall.
It promotes skies.
Maybe one day in the future we
will reincarnate to a place called
the Raven's heaven.

The Might of the
Black Bird Emblem

K5- Kuwait

Tragedy Of Life

The tragedy of life is not
death but what we don't
let go to the spirits.

Our tears, our wounds
created here on earth.

Higher than us.
The act of healing becomes us.
Take the dead to its proper
release at Bûbiyăn.

By these waters,
feed first the ones in the sky.
After the remaining bones are set
a flame,
crush the burnt bones and release
their past to the sea.

Then celebrate their
intermission of life.

Indigenous Burning And Crushing Of Bones

The Poet

Did Kyrgyzstan, think they had the only
poet in mind? Epic Manas, from the people
of Paleo-Siberian stock.
Were once influenced from runic- Turkic
writings, handed down from the bards, may
be the longest written script of 500,000
lines long.
But others have come and gone.
Which highlights, another version beyond.
A different theme of antiquity.
These are the many verses transversely
making up our shamanic history.
Vedic was inclined to be
their interesting blended traditions,
Zoroastrianism was the Pictionary of
their invisible scrolls.
Verbal also became, the stories of other
regions that were once told.
The oral literature of the first clans
that settled near Sulaiman mountains
highlighted the many stories so bold of all of
central Asia.

They said Turkic nation to Turkic nation,
were one example of the many varieties of
tribes that rolled.
Unique became these clans of human
now settled in these regionals zone.

Across the barren silk road,
which illustrates the richness
of each of these countries
hard existence and toll.

Customs so different and intricately deep.
Most people in the West
don't even know that Caucasus
features and even blue eyes slanted
makes up many of central Asia's
exotic mix.
Developed into cultural beauty of
art and poetry, gold covered antiques
of regional glare.
The base words from our history, all clan
dialect diverse, makes up only one component
of this region, to illustrate in this poem Kyrgyz's
beautiful
indigenous flair.
Altin Ara Shan

The One Million Elephants

Our people came centuries ago
from China in the 8th century.
Displacing the many tribes now
disdained as Kha.

Once in the mercy of dark lands
the Khmer Kingdom ruled the
entire region including neighboring
Thailand and Vietnam.

The 16th century onwards our lands
became attractive to Europeans.
We are humble people who still believe
in saffron outfits and the importance
of the Million Elephants at bay.

The Lucky Elephant

Walk Along With Me

Walk humbly with God
the Baltic spiritual way and
kneel, not just in darkness.

You were born the fruits
of labor.
The free men and women
against social injustice.
Don't ever let any blessings
be a dismissal.

A national awakening.
The skies will be your savior,
highest merit are those
born humble with flavor.

Walk along with me.
Your path will be gold and
righteous.

But always remember
pagan and the heavens
were our original ways.

The Gothic scripts of the 16th Century

Roman Style

Baalbek a Phoenician metropolis.
Roma came in 64BC.
And converted the triads of Heliopolis.
Jupiter, Venus and Mercury
from its name of origins
Baal, Anta and Alyn.

What an early monument was erected.
Representing the region known as Sun
worship derived from Greek mythology.
The many pilgrims it attracted to the
metropolis.
An entire city surrounded by
fifty granite-style columns.

Barbaric shamans they had said
"Learn from our ways".
We will never give up our altars
and religious temples, they yelled back.
But aggressive was Roma's impact.

Battle occurred daily in the region.

Converted may have been their historic
point.
Abandoned became their post.
Many new tribes changed over.
The city became permanent,
but the mark of heritage represented the
fierce warriors that are now ghosts.

L4- Lesotho

What Is Death?

The Zulu tribes have attacked.
We expelled them out but darkness
falls over my soul as I stand over
the many graves.

In the middle of winter huddled
together, we take turns looking
blankly in the 4ft deep sloppy
excavated out trench.
Unlike recent times, Thabana
was the preference for their
forefather's burial place.

But gone are my belief in the skies!
An entire family.
How meaningless I think,
as tears pour down my face.

Freezing cold the weather is,
pretty are now the tribally
decorated bodies.

What is death? Weeks I have spent
morning.

When maybe I should celebrate?
And look at it like feeding back
the earth with the souls that are now
departed.

The Hand Of Death

L5- Liberia

Graveyard

I think therefore I am
There must be two of me.
A conscious and a being.

I told those immortal
not to worry!
One was for the sky; one
was for the sea.

In the end I will have left
everything.

Graveyard

L6- Libya

Tour Guide To Tourist

We have so much heritage and
things of interest in Libya.
We also have in Tassili N'Ajjer an
evolution of changes that have
occurred in fauna and flora
over time.

"We are so excited the tourist responds.
Do we get to see written of our earliest?"

Oh no you get to see something even
better he responds. You will see an
order of succession of our first people of
earth and their recorded version of
changes over time on rock paintings.
The rocks of their soul and pain.

When Libya had elephants and
rhinoceros, magic religion scenes
and moist landscapes,
horses and very large plant life.

The oldest images recorded goes
back 14,000 years.

Our earliest forefather's struggles
and a reminder of their existence,
Ottoman politics and their unrested shamanic strife.

Unesco Tassili n'Ajjer Rock Paintings

Homage to Yacoub Aġa

Yacoub acquired a small
plot of land on Sechem and
erected a dolmen.

The brightest star is
the one I wish to follow,
his soul made him desire.

The whispers of my
forefathers before me.
Gave a chill down his
spine.

Surt to Odessa, they roamed.
Though one of the original
12 tribes all were unrelated,
except for one thing.
Unified they became with the
God Yahweh.

Perfection is the one
we desire in us.

Trading for a piece of
bread.
Transhumance for
greener pastures.

Tents we set up
to protect our concubines,
Ones we call our own.

Take a lead Yacoub Aġa.
Tonight you watch
over the many who sleep.

The Holy Bread

L8- Liechtenstein

Liechtenstein	National Holdiay
Our country is small but proud we originate from the Alemani tribe.	We will get more revenue from parties, then we will do having a war. That is why an army is not required in our country this small. On our our national holiday, the serene Prince and Princess invite the entire country to the Vaduz Castle. Smiles and a beer is the flavour, if you have a business plan even better but tears on that day are not authorized at all.

L9- Lithuania

Follow The Path Of Light	The hazy mist sparkles,
It is 3:00 AM and I am in a vast land of green known as the Curonian spit. Trees are hovering over me. Complete darkness in the forest I stay still. The moon is hidden, the single star to the right is what the compass arrow is showing me. The trees whisper to me, *"Dont be afraid"*. Look at this compass, and follow this path of light. The single star glowing, leads me to the edge of the water. The wind blows, and an invisible hands freeze's me all around.	tears pour down. I realize then that I felt those who use to roam here once before me. Follow The Path Of Light Pressured from the Teutonic Knights, we were the last pagan country in Europe. Accepting Roman Catholicism in the late 14th century. Some are ashamed, some are so proud, better late than never the church once yelled.

House of Burgundy

In medieval times, Henry VII
ceded to the "House of Burgundy".
The area once inhabited by all the
Belgic tribes.

Native clans which were part of
the highlands making up the
singing lands of even earlier,
there forefathers the indigenous
of Gutland (utlan).

Many wars ensued.
The Romans, Spanish,
even Germans
came marching right through.

Today its quartier
sits as one of the oldest
fortifications.

A strategically military prize

This is a tiny land with a
written note of heritage.
The building of its people,
many centuries, of history,
science, folklore, art and literature.

The first advancement born from
what the Roman's nicknamed as the
Treveri tribes.

The Treveri Tribes

In Search Of Sanctuary

The kingdom of a very
ancient country.
Part of the Balkan peninsula.
Anatolia and Thrace are its
historic cultures so close.

The locals even have a mix.
A reminiscence of Ottoman influences
in the region.
Albanian, Serbs and Turks join in as their
minorities.

All recite this happy song:

*In every heart there is a room,
a sanctuary safe and strong to
heal the many wounds.*

*Until a new day arises, may God
protect the borders of what we
call our own kingdom.*

*The place heaven made,
what our forefathers
knew.*

The Sun And Spirits

Movement Of First Words

Ada is island in many countries
a word even found in Africa.

Cas is flexing of muscle of the ones
flying and found in South America

Gar means the mountains in
certain parts of Russia.

Kara globally means spirits of darkness

Merge together you get the etymology of the
earliest phonetics out of Madagascar.

Satanically translated,

The strength of the ones flying will be
found on the hilltops of this isle.

Is this a fluke or is this a coincident?
Only an attempt to merge DNA with migration
of phonetics way in the future will tell us?

The Hills Of Madagascar

M3- Malawi

Bettering Thy Self

My greed swallows
me; I need the whole lot I say.

Ignore everything around me.
Diseased with survival,
is the only thing on my mind,
the ravens have betrayed

My family is in disarray.
My children refused to stay.
An infection has taken the best
of me.

A quiet hill on top of the
world. I ask the spirits please
help me, I can't handle this twirl.

The wind touches my face.
Grass tingles my feet,
a soul gently speaks:

*We come to this earth with
a purpose, a call.*

*Why do you feel you have to have it all?
This is a tiny reminder, write it out if
need.
When you depart believe me,
you will have nothing at all.*

My tears I dry rapid
and bury my head in tender.
Oh spirits I say I was
not thinking about
the afterlife thunder.

*You are right
we are not here long,
I will heed your words of wisdom and
wipe my tears, this death omen
does not mean we are forever gone.*

The Focus On Quality

M4- Malaysia

The Language Of Birds When we think of early humans and the role of language historically. Meaning the unknown or hidden dialogues of anything prior to 10,000 BC. Academia wrote it off as just babbling. Today the world was told we are all a reminiscent of shaman! A constant that once existed. Don't believe the message from the souls that are unrested? We will now say don't be radical of your past. Even a Malaysian Blue-Rumped Parrot with its minuscule bird brain can speak human dialect.	Bue Rump Parrot

M5- Maldives

Stars Of The Indian Ocean The hundreds of islands in the Indian ocean tells us one important thing about history. *The journey of life and existence, its beauty and vulnerability, and at night the sparkle of its illuminated Sea Stars had to have started off only by the magic of the heavens and skies.*	Glowing Sea Stars

M6- Mali

Emperor of Songhai

Mohammed was the founder of the
Askia dynasty in 1495.
On his way to Mecca he was so impressed by
the Egyptian pyramids he decided to construct a
tomb for himself.

Upon my death, I want the people of these
Regions to remember me as the King of the
Saharan Gold trade.
A genuine royal representing Africa and its
people.

Emperor Songhai

M7- Malta

The Purpose Of All The Prophets

The island 6000 years back, contained
seven megalithic monuments. The representation
of the development of
first culture.

The famous sites at the time were so holy
that these Malta stones, can even be found in
Anatolia.
Blessed to these structures they were brought as
blocks and carved delicately with care.

Reforming beliefs of those of animals?
We are confused. The Carthaginians had once
asked:

"*What purpose do you hold here*"?

Each time period brings in another,
the locals responded. You came so that we can be
your salvation.

Think about it, what the world was like?
Let go of your emblems and violent ways
and believe in us.

The rocks represent our devotions.
We are a dominant empire of the region.
What purpose do the many prophets from the
region contain?

The Carthaginians continued.

They teach us, that there were numerous people
of divine and they are still here but only in their
spirits, the souls of what was once revered is still
felt today.

We always profess in our hearts, may those who
rule us for wisdom, always be guarded.

The Many Prophet

M8- Marshall Islands

White Star

The 24 points in the median of
stars represent all our islands.
The sparkles from the skies
shines on each one individually.

Our people once had said
Ratak or Ralik?
Indigenous we are, we still do our
daily spirit communications.

In the morning at Sunrise Ratak,
in the evenings at sunset Ralik.

But it is our single White Star that
shines on all the isles that holds
our forefather's destiny.

M9- Mauritania

Cross The Gibraltar

Cross the short strait of Gibraltar
and then use the caravans to reach.
There you will find the fertile
valley, a safeguard and resting spot
to hide the goods, we just brought
over.

Its ancient routes you can use,
to find the oasis trading post so
do not worry.
You wont miss it, the basin is
always clear.

By Ouadane's decorative entrance
you will find a papyrus note.

Follow clearly the directions and
give them the goods.
Take the message the messenger
from the other side has sent.

The map will lead you to the
treasures of gold.

Ancient Ksour of Ouadane

M10- Mauritius

The Extinct Dodo Bird Steal one egg from a Dodo and you can feed five. Steal three eggs from a Dodo throw in some herbs and rock smashed banana you can then feed twenty. The white man came now we can't feed any. This is a true story of how locals lost so many.	The Extinct Dodo

M11- Mauritius

In Aapravasi Ghat the British did the greatest experiment of all time, the site was the place to use what they called "free labour" instead of slaves. We are now called free indentured workers!	

M12- Mesopotamia & North Africa

Babi-illim Our Watchtower (Babylon) Your structure closest to the sky, hovering in the horizon. The ideals of our earliest, be our watchtower. Your shamanic name means our door to enlightenment. This light may it house our fears. We feed the skies ban, we sacrifice for knowledge.	The land of Shinar, and still darkness falls over our watchtower. May the animal fat candle in your top tower be the call to follow Babi-illim. Speak of the lessons of earth, and bless us with the road to the skies, the light and the tower. Babylon's Historic Name – Earliest Meaning Door To Enlightenment.

Transformed Fig Leaf

Fruits of our tree,
relish its sweetness we eat.
The symbolism of life,
the gift of fertility made you real.

Dear child,
how you were born with care.
Naughty are you today.
Sweet like sugar,
rambunctious like a baby lion cub.

The stems are the tussle
that binds your mother's hair.
The leaves are customs
of love that we do not tear.

Dear child,
product of a real warriors' fruitfulness.
The symbolic leaves of figs,
the average doesn't know!

Made Europe turned the symbol of
leaf to a heart for your loving beaux.

You are my ancestry today.

Transformed Fig Leaf

M14- Mexico

The Collapse Of Mayan

Region is Yucatan, 300AD.
The weight of the Gods are
so heavy.
We grind forest hallucinogenic
drugs to ease our pain.
The average age of our
elders are no more than 20.

We pray, help us!
We have exceeded the carrying
capacity of existence.
Droughts are heavy,
and disease has started to
flourished.

Delicate is our soul.
Afterlife we do believe in.
Lets us all agree and do a
blood sacrifice to the Gods.
Find a spare spot each.

And say hello to those before us.

So when we reincarnate,
our lives will not be
in such pain.

Gone did we become
yesterday.
The pyramids are the
death monuments
that will still await our new stay.

The Pantheon Of Nature Gods- Uxmal

M15- Mexico

Chihuahua are our people, how we would have dance, the Maize dance!

M16- Micronesia

Agana

When the sleeping women awakes these mountains will move.

The lead of all vagina's.

The Meat Of A Walnut

Take a walnut it is moist, wet
and raw inside.
Plant it and out comes the
tree.
This tree knows it roots;
and that it was born
from a seed.

It harbours the meat of
those who eat it.
Why is its meat so
important?

Other than all the benefits
of nutrition it provides.
It represents a brain.
When de-shell and not
in disguise.

This brain represents
humanity you see.
You came as humans,

from a single seed.

This is now the analogy
of defining what is human
utilizing a root and a tree.

*The walnut came out of its shell
And did not like its shell.*

Was the amusing irony of race dissection
historically.

The Human Analogy

Honour Thyself

If we were hated by
an army of million,
we wouldn't care.

We know our faith
our destiny.

Honour ourselves.
In all of delight.
By the Grace of
God's will.

With reputation
we built our royalty.

The land of activity
everyday of the
year by the sea.

With no airport there.

Centre Of The Hunic Empire

Temujin has united all the
Mongol tribes.
One noble will be chosen to marry
Musa's daughter, his friend.

Hand to hand was she given after
The defeat of the Tatars, followed
by the great entry into the
Persian Gulf.

Master warriors were all of them
in fight, arches vigilantly developed.
Large stallions groomed with care.
The merging of the two leaders
became their sacred promise.

To control the dynasties of all
the surrounding kingdoms,
were their mottos.
They travelled by horse many
vast lands.

*Death and vengeance struck one
down.*

Musa's daughter then produces 7 more.
The spirit of his friend was now
Restored.

*(Dedicated to My warrior son, Temujin. In
English Teymor)*

Genghis Khan (Temujin)

Black Mountains

The Black mountains, the old region
known as Karst.
Talk to us what have you seen?

Our earliest buried food under
ground, cracked were their hands
with no shovels.
Fingernails of dirt and splinters.
By the fresh water outlets
they would sleep.

They would ask us, oh spirts of darkness
to be kind to their humble souls!
Oh how we would be ruthless and have
fun with all of them.

Back then our mountains had
a different name.
The Venetians came and switch
the game.

The cycle of life is funny you see,
the Ottomans marched in 1389, and
mixed up all their cup of tea.

World War One and Two,
we have seen it all.

We are just the Goblins of Dark
who just keeps carrying away,
the spirits of death.

The Blackened Mountains, All Ten Fingers For
Prayer To Them.

Gua, Hua or Dua

Dear friend you travel so many miles.
Your faith is so different from mine.

But yet you show interest
in Dua, what possess thee?

"God is the same", she replies
We cross all lines to make
a difference.

You need prayer in your life.
It is same message but different
formats, that is really ok.
I will change my Hua to Dua
just for this visit I do here.

Dear tourist all the way from
Central America. Your Amerindian faith is so
different from mine.
But yet you show interest in
the mosques we have here.
What possess thee?

"The structures are all different", he replies
we historically have cross many boundaries of war
over religion,
but today I would like to respect
your house of God.
I kneel my head, like you. We can merge our prayers
together".

For you just this week, I will change my
ancient spirituality of Gua to Dua.
Just for the visit I do here.

Dear Student all the way from Botswana,
our faith's are so similar.
But yours is a different sect and has culturally
different customs than mine.

Come into this little mosque this time.
My African friend politely declines.
Let me try to convince you otherwise.

For many years,
I have brought in many people to this
family run bed and breakfast by the water.
I have never been on a plane, have formal education
or have really left town.

Continue

This area is all I know.
 	
But I want to teach you, how I have been educated from the many who come and go.
 	
    I have learnt that strangers can hold remarkable
    kindness.
    I have seen tolerance of differences
    beyond the told.
    I have learnt from the many young and old.
    Stories of different cultures around.
 	
But what I have learnt most is that Gua, Hua and Dua became God's transitional prayers which are centuries old.
 	
All you need is God in spirit, never forget the story of what this old man just told.	

M22- Mozambique / Mocambique

Portuguese Maritime Routes In 1497 Manuel l asked Vasco da Gama we need a trade route stop to help us with some exchanges with India. The fortification on the island became a resting point. Once fully occupied they returned to Lisbon, laden with shiploads of gold. When gold became limited, Human labor became the new bold.	Fortification St. Laurent

Unpolluted In Our Spiritual Ways

Burma's virgin jungles.
One illnesses and its living
soils will consume you.

The jagged Arakan mountains,
scored by steep river valleys.

Burma's geographically critical point,
sea ways, and war strategic history.

The Pearl Harbour link.
Ping ponged between,
Japan and England continuously.

Burma's people the cleanest
of the clean, living on its golden lands.
Powered by its ancestral spirits
and the will of its people, oh
so grand.

They would always chant:

The purple mountains the
vibrantly blue seas.
The wings covered some days
by foggy clouds.

Mentally connect us continuously
to the heavens.
The awakening of our souls.

We don't mind visitors but we are
spiritually very unpolluted.
Please don't permanently stay,
unless you follow our holiest of ways.

A depiction of a holy shamanic mountain and the
core of earth.

The Beauty Of Raw

Indigenous you are,
your mountains of pain
called Kalahari.

Roots you pull,
for a handful of water.
Meat you steal from cheetahs.
Bush men,
You have a very raw
tribal beauty.

The land tells us
your part of humanities
earliest ancestry,
called the first clans of
earth.

Sing to the skies,
we can only wonder.
The vision of darkness,
in your path that
was once way past yonder.

The nights of no lights;
the cold with no heat.
How did you survive
natures horrible defeats?

Diagram Depiction of Bushmen

Don't You Ever Lose The Fight

Don't you ever, ever give up.
Even in your darkest moments
of the ocean's swell.
Ride that seven years of misery
known as the black side,
the yin's, incursion to the yang of hell.

Did you think an angel was
born without its counterpart.
Wear your tribal masks.
This is the normal combination
of our karmas of past life.

When the clouds of darkness hits.
And the mind has gone.
Run quick to a love one and
let them grip both your arms.
Don't you dare, scream through.
Make sure they also fiercely shake you.

A loving hand, can ward off anything especially
when an omen sends in its devil after you.

Feel your beating heart,
our forefathers would once say.
As the blood rushes by,
these are the normal difficulties,
that everyone has to go through.

The design of life is simple it was
meant to confuse you.
Be understanding,
everyone struggles just like you.
There are no exceptions to this rule.

Don't you ever lose the fight.
A test of survival for the next.
Just remember we are all God's children,
and her spirit in the skies really does loves
you like the rest.

The Spawns of Hell

Mountains Of Pain

Heee- Mal-Aya we pray to you...

The skies, the spirts, the moons
of our very first.
What is the most important in
terms of spiritual beliefs,
we ask of you?

The after life, obviously!

Through their chants, the mighty
spirits would speak back.

Erect you will do the special number.
In shamanic belief the number seven,
became a holy number of the ones that
use to day by day consume you.

The seven groups of monuments
were erected.
A replica located in the valley
of death.

Good! Its lethal peaks you wont need to
pass through.

Katmandu represented the other point of
Hindi. The landing and earliest transposed
powers of the fiercest of them all.

The mountains, the seven temples and the ones who
can devour you. The light of birth of devotion and
that of our piety in terms of highest powers.

Now became a cremation site and its earliest
shamanic beliefs will now be an idle for you.

The Stars and Our Hi-Mal-Aya Mountains

Masters Of The Virgo

We are passionate fearless
forces of art.
Medieval, Tulips, Sadness
All play the part.

Low is our sea land
we shade in.
High are the peaks,
we colour paint.

The wind delicately moves the
windmills, these painters have
made with flowery shades.

Pain reflects the crosses of
designs.
The real life stories of
our past.
Filled with angelic divine.

The old the new, each
era of copycat artists,
their passage of time needed
to pass the wintery landscapes.

Art may be part of our spirits
but wine is the accessory to
help our imagination flow.

We have all become
"Masters Of The Virgo".

N5- New Zealand

The Flightless Bird

Ancient flora and fauna,
a region known as heaven.
What happened to you Takahe?
Do you not wish to fly like the
rest of us?

Did God punish you in a past
life, that you can't look down
at those below you?
Join us we would say.

He answers back.

*Ancient Gondwanaland were my forefather's
regions.
The divine blue falls, the gullies, the mountains
make me stay. Why would I leave paradise and
maybe fall prey?"*

Leave me be, I simply prefer to stay.

Rare Flightless Takahe Bird

N6- New Zealand

Taumatawhakatangihangakoauauotamateapokaiwhenuakitanatahu hills are my home

N7- New Zealand

The Mythical Land Whanganata

Ulu were once your holy mountains
that you would pilgrimage too.
Where do you go now,
Maori people?

We are brave,
But the numbers that come
can hurt us.
We have permanently settled in the outreach,
the smaller inlet of the two.

Your dances of fear,
and face all made up
in animal gear.

Do you fight back
Maori people?

No, they all smile.

We stick out our
warrior tongues,
and make lots of noises.
They then leave us
real quick.
This is our way.

We are known as the fearsome tribe.

Maori Warrior Sticking Out Tongue

N8- Nicaragua

Niiii They Screeched

Half naked they bend over to drink.
The moon glistens on the holy black lake
they called Nicaragua.
No different than God's water in India
Just 50,000 years earlier.

Niii they also use to screech!

Niii

N9- Niger

The Aga Of The Region

The Hausa people they would say:
Until the hunt is in favour of the lion,
the hunter or king will always be the lead
Aggg of its territory.

I travelled to India, where I live with my other
African brothers who have lived in India for
centuries, only to find out in there local Kannada
languages they also would say:

Until the hunt is in favour of the lion,
the hunter or king will always be the lead
Aggg of its territory.

The Lead

N10- Nigeria

White-Face Painted, African Tribe

Your color may be the same,
but you are from the other side.
Fierce is your battles.
Trust we have not.

Your appearance may be the same,
but you are from the other side.
Our language is different,
for our protection.

Your women we do crave,
but you are from the other side.
Come we take them and
kill you to pieces.

Your land is harsh but we can
still use, we never forget
you are from the other side.
Only one white face clan can
survive.

African brothers,
Ibo, Kanuri, Hausa, and
Yoruba tribes
are to mention the few.
We are merely ten minutes away,
yet we are not the same,
you are from the other side.

The Dancing Tribes

Negroid

Are you offended that
I call you the darkest of them all.

Picked violently from Chad, Niger, Sudan
on feces infested boats.
The blaring sun was your only
naked coat.

The house and the field
separated you,
the scars and battles
wounded you.

The fruits of the this
world made you sweet.
It was man that got confused
and try to make you weak!

Ill mannered is not
that bliss.

When we look at the
damages on our
historical list.

Are you offended that
I call you the darkest of them all.

Don't be, it is a replica of
Humanities ignorant mist.

Bedouin Indigenous Female

Clan female!
Decorate yourself so beautiful,
for our first night.

Always cover yourselves.
We have many men
from miles away
that can sense your
virginity.

Go get water in
groups.
We will protect you till death.

You carry the life of our
ancestry.
We know once they touch
you we would have lost our
forefathers.

Clan female!
Protecting you, means
protecting our genes,
that will carry us through.
Only we can touch you.

Bedouin Indigenous Female

Forested Shaman

In spirit do I see,
an outline of glass,
foggy white in nature.

Forested shaman
where do you hide?
Your bones are only
left in sacred sites.

Let your suckers of life,
come back through to us.
And now be the tips
of the tree tops.

Forested Shaman
Why do you howl to us?
Let your essence finally rest.
We will now connect with
you in spirit and nature.

Forested Shaman

N14- North America's Natives

Great Spirit In The Sky

Oh great ancestry,
we call on you.
The moon, the spirits, the earth.
We were born
free.

From the same mother.
Sacred is our rock,
pain is our rituals.

Oh great ancestry,
life is the soil under our feet.
Look at the sky.

Our connection will
always be to you.
Calls to you are made
to lead us to
the Hee's in the skies.

Shamanic we sing,
out to you!
Hiawatha now a leader,
of a great spirit.
We bow to you.

Where There Are Feathers, There Were Shamans

N15- North America's Native

We have officially healed,
we just wrote off humanity
and called it a day!

Healing

Man, Women And Child

The blood of a female
soaks into the moss,
between her private.

Picked delicately from the top of
stones, that harbour the moss.
It has always been pressed and
dried softy in
the shade known as heaven.

§

The child's excretion,
wiped outside with snow.
Its small body
becomes slightly frozen.

Until mother and child
are hidden under the
heavy leather caribou
tarp, the child keeps crying.

§

The man's wounds
an omen from a wild
animal's kick.

Healed with a birch and plant
mix.
Medicine a shaman doctor
has provided.
Man, women, child are the
    extensions of earth.
The Circle Of Life

N17- North Korea

Blessings & Misfortunes

In a time of earthly devastation
what does one hand
say to another?
Come let me help you.
We are human in design.

In time of abundance
what does one hand
say to another?
Stay the way you are, and agonize.
This is self preservation.
We are still human in design.

The difference is simple
if you can see.
One is an omen collectively from the skies.
The other is internally coded in early human
creations.
Of the need to subdue and
the existence in beings.

Centuries old behaviours and
ancient are these encoded social
codes of genetics.

The key is breaking a perception
and what is better always for both
you and me.

N18- North Korea

Once upon a time Koreans of common blood
lived as clans in small groups; then their tribes
got bigger.

Now their people are a homogenous race mixed
with other Turkic, Mongolian and Tungustic
(Tun-gush) people all belonging to the Altaic
group of languages.

Yi Admiral Sun-sin

Darkness And Ice

Male is the land we walk on.
Blonde and giant we are.
Made fierce from the ice covered land.
Norse is the power that makes us
stand tall.

We tell the world,
we don't give a shit who's
forefathers we bear.
Animal was before us.
Made by God was each child
crafted and our own.

Compare us to no others,
we don't accept any.
Christian Scandinavian
centuries old,
is what was picked up.
Culture we ride with might.

We rise high and proud,
we are Norsemen till death,
may you tell the skies?

Norway's Outline

The Nor-Way Is The Path

Our first settlements by the
shore are dated at 5,000 $_{BC}$.
Germanic became the brothers
of our stock.
Comprised of Baltic, Alpine and Nordic.

Our clan were chieftains and warriors
different from the rest.
Our women so strong, even gave
birth in snow.
The matter of life, mixed with the blood of cold.
Our first got molded from our land, our
children of the snow.

Year after year our earliest indigenous
used raw hands on ice, to lumber or fish.
Tempted to live was our fight to exist.

The northern skies,
the Nor-way now became our
path of light,
This is exactly how we were born.

Our proud heritage past and what we
call our home.

The Northern Light

The 21 Tombs

In the early morning hours
one of our youngest was
sacrificed.

Hardship on the land was
the reason.
We were sure we had done
something wrong.

The eldest decreed death
to him.
Ghostly white was his colour
and we were sure the skies
would prevent omen once
they reaped all the benefits.

Our funeral practices are different
from others. We can only feed
them and place their bones after
seven moons, on the eve of sunset.

Beehive shaped is our graves and
the vengeance the skies cast on us
is dedicated to our females,
our monumental praying towers.
But first we sing:

Al Ayn chant again
Al Ayn
Al Ayn

May spirit of the spirit return and bless these
lands and our steeple called Al Khutm.

The 21 Tombs

— P —

P1- Pakistan, Northern to India	P2- Pakistan, Northern to India

The Kafirs Of Hindu Kush

By the Hunza river, how we prayed.
Animalist indigenous was our cliché.
Utler is our region, how the ones flying
control our ancient shamanic ways!

The British once overly enjoyed their stay.
But so did the Greeks, Chinese, and
Persians

Beautiful are our women, the stories
of their lives alone can be made
into a historical essay.

Blue Eyed Brown Skin Child

The Regions Of Kashmir

Dark skin, blue eyes.
Native your people
still are.
A rare phenotype but this time
not distinct to one person.
Groups of them, makes these
people distinctive in style.
How beautiful these human are!
Even Alexander the Great once had
said.
> Carry a few females back home
> It's their piercing eyes
> some will be bred
> Our children they will store.

Kashmir was one territory of its original people. Uttar was the other. The landing point are its pain riddled mountains. Ancient were there ways, they once freely roamed. One sect of our earliest humans carrying blue eyes. The earliest indigenous transformations of permanent blues on earth. Call them earths rarity, designed by the heavens in its rarest form. A n interesting genetic social display.

P3- Palau	

Question: Why did the shark not eat the indigenous by Kayangel?

He knew the waters were abundant with fish and he could share.

The Cleaners of Our Seas

We Are First Clan

We are first clan
indigenous in nature.
Born on this land.
Living with the other brown Jews,
for centuries always offering a hand.

Out came the blonds
and attempted to assert
themselves on our holy lands.
They said something about an exodus,
that my friend is silly.
These were their summer homes.
Who merged with the few left after the
Holocaust but in reality Palestine
was ours to house the many.

The Answer
     We are also first clan!
     Do not be fooled by the
     quick change over in colour.

Slavery dispelled us from our own
territories.
North Africa and the entire Anatolia

What do you mean do not mutter?

The Answer
     Fine think as you wish.
     We came and took like others,
     What do wish to do?

Palestine

became the range of our earliest Jews.
Kazar's are what you must be
referring too?
For centuries we asked the sultans to
give us a small plot of land.
And then there are the many
archaeological finds,
that should be enough evidence there.
mutter.
This was God's call, what he declared.
As for the Exodus this is true, are you dispelling our
will?
We laid the holy rock first,
this is our land, please do not

The Response

The land was not owned once upon
a time. Lies you do you are only Europeanized;
do you think we are fools?

We are no different, than the tragic tale of north
American Native too. For centuries we were here
with the original Jews. We had an Ottoman
neighborly bond, our saddest journey and woe
became born when it was gone.

                    Continue…

P5- Panama

Green Canopy Tops

Hanging off my balcony,
all I see are the green tree tops.
Living do they colour the skies,
screaming are the noises,
that come out of them.

My world is coloured,
like the vibrancy of colour in them.
Foggy and dew filled in design.
Hand painted from the heavens,
green are our canopy tree tops.

Gualaca Panama

P6- Papua New Guinea

The Lord Of The Flies

We march through the hardest
of swamp lands called Inanwatan.
We have no elders our tribes
are made up of predominantly many
young adolescents barely reaching
of age.

Ten thousand years ago,
our favourite foods were
banana and yam.

When others attack we fed
them to the skies.
But before we did, the leads
got the heart, we only got the hands.

The Soul Of An Enemy

Indigenous We Are

Potato Yucca and Yam
We crush with our feet.
Indigenous we are.
A love we have,
in sharing when we eat.

Mestizo, Ache, and Chiripa
is our local people.
The first on the land
that would speak.
Descendents of Guran.

Their spirits they would
recount of that in the sky,
that would always be watching
the harvesting season that went by.

Culture beyond the moons.
Is what we sing.
Home to our active
God Amamba,
the destruction of
what she can brings.

Indigenous we
are when we tap.
Help us compress
our starches for
our winter fest.

It helps the time
go by faster so we
can dance.

Potato, Yucca and Yam.
Watch us prance.

Guaran People

Peruvian

Spaniard you came,
so much blood,
on your hands.
You dressed us shut and
said we were not even a man.

Spaniard you forced.
Ancient skies were once our beliefs.
Suddenly a white man, blue eyes,
over time was the one
that gave us relief.

Battles so fierce,
we quietly knew you had won.
But something happened
an irony of the past gun.

We merged old with new,
one generation after another.
More like 500 years later.
This was a part of history's funny
maneuver.

Today even if we wanted to go
back, we would fight you violently!

Spanish nights became our
Peruvian style.
Feverishly colourful in design
was now our flavour for
everyone to see.

Spanish-mix indigenous,
became our forefathers evolved.
Grown from our historical wounds,
an emergence of culture with love.
We personally don't focus about the ethics
of past, in all this jive.
A heart which burst through our shirt can now
be seen, that Hispanic today has become our
national pride.

The Flaming Heart

Nonbeliever

Let's discuss the difference
between a nonbeliever and one
that magnifies God's name.

Nonbeliever, accept all oblations since
God had to have given existence,
and therefore judges all truth.

You know all the moral,
Palawan long, Marianna trench deep
kind of stuff.

The one closest to hell,
that carries immense depth.
That doesn't scare you.

Nonbeliever, does this bore you?
Probably so, but ironically
only in despair, when your pain is
unbearable and your darkest anguish
comes to light.

Do you ignore your thoughts of reason,
and scream out for anything that
could be a savior.

Nonbeliever, offer what he abominates.
Heal yourself with what the skies
and the energies of what the cosmos
has to offer you.

One-day morality and judgment may
reincarnate you.
My advice to you, don't take chances.
Since being balance, or that of equilibrium, are
the laws
of all the universes.

Spirituality And Faith

The Churches Of Peace

The significance of the basis of morality.
What if I told you God exists, would you be
morally correct?
What if I told you God doesn't exist,
would you be morally correct?

Philosophical as it may sound the
question to humans then becomes:
*Should we or shouldn't we think,
to be socially and morally correct?*

The basis of morality therefore shouldn't be
dependent on that of the possibility of the
questions of God.

Entrenched into ideology of centuries old,
Jawor, the invading armies to the pagan people
of the region would say, do you actually question
honour and the skies?

Remember the revelation of angels
dictates a real examination of the one above.

Faith

Boats in the harbour 1830.
Long dangers of voyage
to new exotic places.
Fado recite to us history about
the sadness of our early voyage,
missing home and
their longing for their comfort places.

Socialist reforms and
radical propaganda
became Lisbon's darkest censorship.
Fado tell us a political story about
what was done in 1929.

Folk dances, long dresses.
Catholicism push to heal.
Fado sing to us your old
rural songs of saddens, romance,
cultural heritage.
An entire nation struggles and
tunes of different human ordeal.

The epoch has entered 2000 and they
are still proud Fado singing
Portuguesismo.

The Royal Tribe, Bani Tamim

The Portuguese in the 1500's were the worst, to our earliest people in Catara. An attempt to make a fortification failed horribly.

Then came the migrating Al Khalifah people in the 18th century who started relocating to North western Qatar, the Persian's immediately felt threaten and invaded it stationing troops in the region.

We were actually happy under Persian rule because they accepted our local people's names of shamanic beliefs and even intermixed with us. They also taught us honour. We were only one tribe of family then of approximately 50,000 people.

In 1914 the British during Ottoman came and created a treaty that sheltered us as a protected state.

It took several years but thank God we gained our own liberation in 1971.
The virtue of freedom gave us the blessing of an independent state.

Bani Tamim

R1- Romania

Drakula

We are the first.
Seven represents our holy
number of death.

We cut its throat let it bleed
and drink to be men.
A form of aphrodisiac by the entire
tribe.

This has been the core of shamanic
living since way back then.
Dracula

Our seven villages inscribed and
founded by the Transylvanian Saxons
has existed since Middle Ages.
We make sure all our churches are
in fortress format.

Our legend today still rings through as the one
who drinks blood.

A Goblet of Blood

R2- Romania

Bucharest is our capital today, but hear he.
To the beauty of the skies, we also once use to fly.

R3- Russia

Catherine The Great

Many lovers do I have.
A symbolism of force.
A Europeanize heritage I
gave to Russia.
Make love do I do,
to broker a peace treaty with
the Ottomans.
The year is now 1774.
Annex our land we make up.
Split our land we separate 1787.
A circle now designed by an enemy's mate.
Let's try this again my lover that I enjoy.
Flamboyant I am, you are my toy.
Annex our land we make up.
Split our land, one final clash,
before we forever go 1792.
Russia needs a foothold in
the black sea my advisors
are told.
Austria is also our enemy,
the Crimean Peninsula,
in a position so bold.

Build up the navy
in the greatest of way.
For the towns and small cities.
Russia will now forever stay.
Livid I am at their Ottoman Empire,
I have no mercy.
Loyalty they want from me,
but promiscuous are my curvy tools.
Catherine the Great I am, they
must be totally confused.
They want me tame,
like an animal locked in a zoo.
Who the hell are these
clans, unlike others.
They are socially funny in design
watch them pray.
I won't sin with an opposing other.

They will learn the hard way
at my inner strength,
I will defeat their armies and show them
I am no damn fool!

Catherine The Great

R4- Russia

Out of this chaos emerged Russia, whose victories at Khazan freed their country of their Tatars dominations.

Different Tribe / Same Dialogue Battle

One to One…did they battle

The Passageway Of Energy

Large masses of energy once past through God's
hand on earth.
A few Venus' he laid claim,
to breed.

The shamanic might
of first women.
The drawings of life
hidden in a Denisova Cave.

They are our females,
to think about.
They were called the

Mother's of earth for
a reason.

Energy is the spirit they
gave to each head of
clan that roamed;
in the darkness of the
vast plains.

Feeding the spirits through
their breast,
became their magnificent
capacity for existence.
The energy channel of life
from one soul to another.

Power Source

R6- Russia, Yakut

The Circle Of Life

The lengthy migration has halted.
The hundreds of reindeers on this
vast green plain now simply
circle continuously.

Even the token rare white
one, looks so well blended in.
Our special spirit, the Natives
once would say.

A large buck, would be our eye
marker in following the full rotation
of this circular motion.
Viewing them on top of the plains.

Man needs not look
at sciences but rather what
our own surroundings give us
in terms of information.

Chemicals they spew continuously
not realizing in the end all of it goes
back to the basics. This circle of life.

Our earliest forefathers would
study the variety of
magnetic pulls of earth.

No different than the irony of this
herd and a single white buck twirling
around in a daze.

They would attempt to make
sense of the world they lived
in then.

A prayer of blessing of what is
indigenous and their traditional
knowledge's past on today.

The Prayer of Indigenous Traditional Knowledge.

Fierce Child

Hands so small,
yet dry blood is filled
under your nails.

When you should be
really playing with toys.
Lost in the confusion
of the scars you bear.

The omen of social
ills brought forth
from primitive man.

Ripped becomes
your tiniest body.
Amongst men
that man you.

Fierce child,
forgive humanity
for not protecting you
today.
Dedicated to children soldiers.

The Drastic Mistake Of Early Man

Dead today, your lush forests
are now gone.
Once home to an infestation
of hominids.
Lively were your animals in the streams.
Oh Sahara how much damage has our earliest
people of earth done?

Variety of creature's in disguise,
from tree to tree.
Continuous water vapour,
a splendour of mist to see.

Multitude of colour was what housed
the spectrum of rainbows because
of the life it stored.
Called the compost breathing on dead clay
grounds, and treetop singing sparrows.

Then primitives, slowly but truly transformed
this land.
Humans now became the display of earth.

The dominant start of settlement and that of
early man.
An attempt to cultivate the arid terrain.
The failure of soil became our horrid disarray.

In all of our history, nothing was fiercer than
then the pulling of life from the land.
An intricate underground network,
called the vital component of earth.

The dead now became our inherent and
continuous environmental battle, the gradual
transformation to an arid wasteland.

It all started with domesticated animals, the
source of food and the extra helping hand.

Animals were used to remove the roots called
the suckers, the living beneath the land. Roots
of bushes were dried and laid. Trees eventually
started to fade away.

Our first heating became the only way.
Chocked became vegetation, the tiniest became
the pockets that stayed.

Continue…

<u>*Continue*</u>

Battle of forces to what dwindled,
a drastic mistake of earth was clearly made.

Listen to these words carefully of what our
primitives would once say. There are 900 million
square miles, look for land, and fire fuel Sah-ara
(Sağara).
This was our earliest struggles and shamanic
ways.
The first words of our forefather's whispers a
completely different story for us today.

Over time reminiscent of everything living on
its soil disappeared. Swallowed and broken up
by the breakables. Called the fluctuating weather
and harsh tumbler sands. Compounded heat
grew, now became the tumor of our ancestral
lands.

Man now looked for alternatives. The black-shale
in earth's cracks moved from second to first in
command.

Mother earth damaged nothing left over to last.
Dead became the region, it changed all our maps.

Caribs

When visited by Christopher Columbus he said "the Caribs are warlike and cannibalistic in nature. We need to humanize them. I will name this Island after one of the fourteen holy helpers. Sankt Christopher, the Patron Saint."

The seas are rugged we get violently
green and sick.
When at night we go to sleep,
Fourteen angels watch over us.
Two my head are guarding,
Two my feet are guiding;
Two upon my right hand,
Two upon my left hand.
Two who warmly cover
Two who o'er me hover,
Two to whom 'tis given
To guide our steps to heaven.

We will pray.

The Caribs

The Volcanoes That Spoke

Look inside,
the Piton's are hungry.
Throw one more in.

If you madden them
they will spit immense heat.
Stay very still
and pray to them.

They are our faceless men.
Their anger makes us
steer clear, only when we suffer
we know its time to feed.
Oh the brew-ha of mayhem.

The medicine man in the tribe
is the only one who can see them.
The rodents and opossums we also
feed them.

Watch them produce the white heat.

Soufriere, St Lucia Volcanoes

S4- Saint Vincent And The Grenadines

Amerindian Worship We have found an altar which shows worship on the island. We are able to communicate with them. They say their lives depended on the great spirits from above, and that they prayed in secret each sunrise. They told us a story about why they held a polished black rock in their hands. The idea that they can be strong like the sacred black rock.	The Blessed Black Polish Rock

S5- Samoa

Tutuila We sing to the skies, for we were all ocean born. We pray to the heavens for our land teaches us the skies merciless blows. We dance around our dead for they will come back as spirits untold. Ut Ut, Ulu or Ula the father, ghost and Holy son prayers our earliest shamans globally told.	Region Pago Pago, Samoa

S6- San Marino

Ave Maria

The sounds, our surroundings once
bestowed to our humans.
They included the start of
refine words and beautiful tunes.

Ut, re, mi, fa, sol, la; Ti and Do

We were against the reformation
to our heavenly Gods.
Our idols and sacrifices to him we did love.
We sang to him, please help us and
destroys all our foes.

Did it work, oh no.

We built on top of this mountain, the
mighty Titan. A castle protective and so bold.
We started creating art, literature and now
composed
today it became…

Do re mi fa so la ti and doe

Our Sky Was Once Owned By
The First People Of Earth.

S7- Sao Tome And Principe

The Land Made Me

I am a chameleon, evolved from the land.
I see therefore my internal just picks up the many
colours of my surrounding.

This is called germination and the by-products of
what was given from the land.

S8- Saudi Arabia

We Apologize

In more recent times,
Ottomans did we hate.
But let not for-take,
The reason or
the missing component of
our historical awake.

Our people centuries of an
amalgamation of several tribes.
Persia, North Africa to Anatolia
to name a few.

In the end when those shamans
needed written,
it was our alphabet, prayers
that they raked.

They spread it across
North Africa to Iran.
And did not offer grace.
They called us primitive
thus little is known.

We apologize to the ancestries
of Ottomans for the hotel
we just made of their
old homes.

Cultural heritage will now be
part of our protected zones.

So much history and
differences we have.
That which was written
in stone.

Yes we are different
and do marry,
One, two, three and sometimes four.
This is part of our past, an
indigenous protective score.

Misunderstood by the foreign.
Who are always welcome to stay
but don't even bother or come near.
All of our females are fully owned,
even in the present day.

Today we are shocked to learn when
Rih-yad became our earliest spirits.
Yanbu, Karan, and Dalgan
became a loan.

Al-Alyad Ottoman Fort

In the Battle of Life

Aryan men were designed
from a miniscule speck,
in the spectrum of multitude of colours.
A single molecule,
copied an encoded light.

God's gift to the colour charts.
Purity white in sheer delight.

They too were part of them,
way back then,
in the battle for life.

Not aware in the past,
other colours diluted
each era to the next.

One day a holy apple was
given to a she which,
is now their permanent might.
Today education became,
the supreme, our power of fight.

The key is their genetics
were always there.
Our Aryans, their rare
colour white was
a gift from the very start of life.

The Opposite Spectrums Of Colours and Life

In the Battle of Life

A seed from under earth,
the breaking of soil, our first female.
Became an extension of primary life.
Designed, from the skies onto the womb,
she became "mother first".

An indiscriminate random pick,
in the multitude of colours.
A single molecule of colour,
was picked from the heavenly skies.

This was God's will, a colour
chosen from the charts.
The earliest browns,
now became our sheer delight.

Those that followed inherited
a piece of them, way back then,
this was one part in the
battle for life.

Not aware in the past,
other shades also called the
first colours of earth,
mixed in and diluted,
each era to the next.

These dominants now became
the first clans of earth.
Shaman became thy name.
Roamed for millions of years
In the hunt for game.

The key is their genetics
were always there.
Our almondy browns were
a gift from God, our dominant hues
from the very start of life.

Dances of Life

Resistance is futile
they told the tribes
along the Senegal river.

We clash fiercely
dances till death.
Ululate we called on others.
All alone were we in
the battle during slavery.

Shaman straw dresses.
Foreigners we battle and
felt no mercy,
when we ripped.

Not a bone in our body
for you to catch.
Just a song or two.
To celebrate their defeat.

Famous are our Senegalese
dancers from the very start.

Our leads dressed up
with a mask and a heart.

Try catching us, we will
two-step around you.
We do the dances of life,
and we are not kidding when
we say that to you.

The Seven Ethnic Groups Of Senegal

S12- Serbia

Stari Ras

Deep in the human
psyche, a horrid
weakness exist.

One of fear,
the very human
need to be dominated.
A collection of weight.
That makes the soul
obsessed.

Controlled becomes
our spirits.
Lack of power in
our thoughts is now
our weakness.

Free yourself!
God whispers,
and ease your internal
from all the negative
spirits.

The King of all Hawks,
Uros in 1260 built
these monuments that will
be here to help protect
you always.

King Uros

S13- Seychelles

We land here it is 1609. In this region that I feel
is like the Garden of Eden,

I declare there has to be
a God!

British East Indian Company Expedition

Raven's In The Sky

I carve this ivory stone,
that looks like
a raven.

I think of only one thing
as an African man we posses
one power others don't.
Our impenetrable will.

Raven we call out to you.
You give us our strength.

The pursuit begins.
We follow you so you can
let us know where the water
hole is.
Our hunt for food and some
deerskin.

Remember our impenetrable will.
Oh what songs we will sing.

The Raven Made From Ivory

My Motto Is Balance

In a world so hard
democracy, peace, progress,
justice and equality
is what I ask for.

But when I have a fair
country should there
be actually more?

The eye in the sky
to the depths of hell.
Reciprocal, up and down,
the emotions of our lives
go?

The tightrope walk
is my goal
while keeping a
balanced load.

In my lowest points,
what would life be?

I reach back high to
attain as I try to cope.

In my highest point,
what would life be?
I try to refrain, and instead come
down to enjoy the smaller
tingle of joy.

My motto is balance
as I walk this tightrope.

But once was written in very ancient Javanese
language form. Cited in a different ritual.
Lord Save us, he is the one I pay homage,
in present invisible form.

At the focus of any meditation to heal the
soul will be embodied in both the material and
immaterial wealth of existence from the land we
were born
You will provide the great calm.

Kulamun Durung lugu
Aja pisan dadi ngaku- aku.

S16- Singapore

Our Indian Prince

Centuries ago the people of Malay once said,

Utama is what we should be looking in the skies for.

Our prayers were heard.

The skies then produced a son and he now came to us as the first person of earth in human form.

They called the first in the region born an Indian Prince.

Indian Prince Sang Nila Utama

S17- Slovakia

Is There A God?

Oh skies above
is there a God?

Does he exist
and if there is,
who made God?

The answer is:
Universe to Universe,
Star to Star,
Demän to Demänovska,

Even the underground
world, with its hot-cold caverns
of dark, were built
by the hand of dusted gold.

With the speck of first
stone put by divinity of the
supreme.

Therefore, we enlighten
the many.

Even the God's
had to have had a God
from before.

The Demon In The Karst Cave

S18- Slovenia

The Stilt Houses Of Slovenia

Seven thousands years ago,
at the edge of the rivers or the lakes.
Man left us marks of our early prehistoric
keepsakes.

Glacial was the temperatures with barely
any sleight.
Social development is the highlight of
how advanced our earliest made way.

Our European Prehistoric Villages

S19- Soloman Islands

Darkness

Don't go too deep,
the water is dangerous.
Its suction will pull you in.

It living soul will not protect you.
Instead ride the tides,
in the mornings you will
heal yourself.

And don't go too deep.
There in the darkness
he that rises.

The Darkness In The Tide

Shaman You Are, Shaman I am

Its two years and we have made it to the
tributaries. Tired we are.

What you speak and I speak are relatively
constant. This was the case of what came out of
our animal world.

When phonetics and dialects were the only
variations. No different than the monkey's in
the trees.

Shaman its now 50,000BC! Why are you
completely changing?
the order of your first sentences or words?

Are you protecting your own clan from our
destructive tribes that have started to hunt you in
this breeze?

Hominid Dialogues

In the Light Of The Sun

We called our kings Kral,
the Dutch made it cattle!

Our name of shamanic belief
was San, the British turn us
into wild Bushmen.

Our land was free.
The diamonds and gold rush
in the late 1800's
eventually made our own territory
into the Queen's land.

We wanted to break free of Apartheid
but they put our leader into the horrid pen.

When in reality, if we listen to the
wounds of the earth we were born as
the leads of all of the land.

The Shamanic Sun

S22- South Korea

Many Moons Ago

Once upon a time
humans were all brothers.
In an inlet place they said
proto-Turkic in its advanced
linguistic form was born.
The first marks of life
on the oracle of bones.
This was before the 1400's
time zone.

To Korea many went.
History in search of.
Only to find Hangul's
three kingdoms
were hidden in full dialogues,
pre-enlightenment to the world.

We are the ancient people,
who worship the suns and embrace
the moons.
Let go of your animal kingdom
strife and let the planet bloom.

World powers said no!

Two thousand years ago when these institutions
were set up we couldn't change
these administration point of views.
And yes we did know.

Their books of hundreds of years now
overthrown. We never focused on unwritten and
their linguistic change overs,
to be honest shaman is still very new to us and
unknown.
We do feel very low. Today Korea proudly says:
Humanity has done such a
defeat. Progress is understanding
what is global history. The migratory dialogues
of our earliest and its two million years of
55,000 people's shamanic ancestry.
We celebrate, the skies, the earth
And what it means to just be.....
May the world release doves for global peace.

S23- South Sudan

Once upon a time, more like over 10,000 years
ago. Our land was lush, green and full of water.

The Sons Of Darkness

Spain spoke:

Sons of darkness some of your other
clans must be.
Hebrew is also your ancient alphabet.
Salamanca is your regional dialects.
But why is your beliefs of birds something
you refuse to let go?

What is your choice they continue on and
say:
Death, or expulsion?

To the highest courts we make a command
we will simply do a forced conversion,
something for us that is so delightfully grand!

Christ is our saviour,
to the Yahud believing Jews.
Our churches will now
depict you as a gargoyle.

While the Christian mercenaries
of light peck at your skull
in the hells of fire.
Learn from us the right way.

Today we ask you Spain
tell us the real truth,
behind how recent was
the length of time
to transfer to a monotheistic God?

One of a hidden whispering campaign.

Ci or Si or Sea?

Which Si was meant to be?

Somewhere in a cave
in the coldest point of
the world, early humans
looked for si.

But not the sea they
would like it to be!

In migration they moved to
Siberia, known first as si leri.
By the waters edge in our
Shu-man-ik history.
But this was not the si either,
they would like it to be!

Many died, the ones that
travelled made it.
Hunter gathers
they still moved.

Our earliest first, wandered,
relocated to less
harsh lands.

People of Cieza (Ci-eza)
they became known.
Where their Sea,
the Spanish Si's became
their right Ci.

Holly fresh spring water was this Ci,
lined in order, all hearts open to the sky.
Their Roman fort, became strong,
by the sea.
Centuries later,
It provided us the clues,
to which Ci or Si or Sea was the
people of Cieza's preference for Ci.

City of Cieza Spain

S26- Spain / Italy

Columbus Said

I do not get it.
From East to West.
All I see are
barbaric shamans,
your highness.

How did they migrate
to both lands?
So many Indians I see!

From what I know
Kan-Tan are their
territories,
Kana are some of their people.

These are the first.
But there seems to
be many more.

We have killed
a few dozen.

And extracted a lot,
but we need men.
Lots of men.

Slavery did not work
well with them.
We now eye Africa instead,
we will build and dominate.
Like our forefathers before.

Your highness
if we don't,
we will starve here.
Our people are ghostly white.
We have no heat,
our land is not right

Please give us more
aid.
And lets take over
with full might.

Columbus & Spanish Queen

The Flying Goddess

Thanusha, or mighty one you were born
deep in the heart of Africa,
centuries ago.
Something rattled your spirits.
You travelled all the way
to Sri Lanka.

The land of cattle and Sigir,
our animals of richness and
divine traits.
Do you want to join in?

We have many Gods we
pray too.
What is one more of worship
I ask of you?

The flying Goddess continues
to sweeps around the skies.
You did not answer our
calls.
We ask you again Thanusha!

Maybe we will feed you quick and
run from you.

*"We know you can awaken all life. The power to
create hurricanes or stir all creatures that have
feet, and even make the other birds of air fly up".*

Tan·usha, don't use your might.

We will always acknowledge that you are holy
and great.
Our Goddess in the skies.

The Land of Cattle and Sigir

S28- Sudan

They Asked Nubia?

What is the one thing you can't change they asked the many in Napatan?

The Meroitic speaking from Kushite civilization responded.

The Nubian order of life.
Don't try to accumulate wealth.

You will never win.
These other rulers in the surrounding territories are also large and very parasitic.
And don't want you there.

Stay a humble servant and chattel.
Instead focus on your quality of life.
Don't fall a slave, yet stay simple.
Prioritize your families' chores.

You come to this earth to be our Kingdom's toy.

S29-Suriname

The Lieutenant for the Dutch West India Company said:

The Chinese blacks and the Bosch negroes are not integrating well, see if you can kill some men and intermix their women.

The depiction of real historical slave life, driven by those in power, had once said.

The Intermixing of slaves

The Great River Of Usutu

They have killed or taken many mainlanders. The people from the region of Sena near Zambezi river are now currently moving in.

Happy the land is now temporarily free of the other fractioning tribes.

Many artefacts like pottery and iron, from their homes can still be found.

The Sena locals said we are very confused though, why are these demons calling our peaks, a river now?

Make you Laugh Some More

One, two, three or four, I want to make you smile some more.

Are you Black,
Are you Turkic,
Are you Native,

I asked?
These are the ancestral first of our past!

You must be ill, some Swedes said.
Our monkeys, Neanderthal in type
were bright white and fluffy.

Mix in the intellectual ferment,
genetic purity, is what we carry.
With baby blue eyes of
saturated light.

A quick response came
blaring through,
read this secret research.

Don't be mad please.
This is exactly how I
gently tease!

The concept of being one,
as humans.
Theories on evolution,
whose monkey is better,
What is colour saturation
has humanity all in tears.

Love thy neighbour
laugh some more.
And don't be like others,
from colonial days who simply
wants a score.

What is a human clan,
and now understand the marry.
Educated on DNA ethics is the way,
all of humanity should now be.
Are you Black,
Are you Turkic,
Are you Native,
I re-asked?
Redeem yourself Europe for your craziest past!
Expressionless, they looked.
From something called shamans, and not a stork or Vikings? Today we have become even more confused?
Quick get the scholars to divert this horrid mess. Some of us Swedes are now under major distressed. Two days later this was their very polite address:

The land, filled with snow, made our skins white like china,
the azure of the sea made our eyes brightest of blues,
blonde was the sun converting our hair,
How dare you disrespect centuries of our generational pool.
A huge smile was sent
to their height's above.

Sweden's Christmases

Snow trickles down lightly.
Fireplace burning apple
scents so slowly.
All the mugs painted carefully.
Lil Peter joyfully says:

Papa open the calendar,
let's eat one more chocolate.
Tell me how many
more days till Christmas.

Eighteen more days
Don't let the pine
hurt your small hands.
Help me son lift this tree.

Grand mama open the calendar,
let's eat one more chocolate.
Tell me how many
more days till Christmas.

Fourteen more days.

Patience is the key,
instead light all the candle tips.

Put the last socker around,
A little more time and then it becomes
another year gone.

Don't get that impatience.
Instead help stitch each popcorn
kernel.
Delicately around it goes in the
circle.

Mama open the calendar,
let's eat one more chocolate.
Tell me how many
more days till Christmas.

Seven more days.
All the glass
ornaments are up.
Help put the shimmery
sparkles, use the step stool
to get to the ones on top.
Grand papa open the calendar,
let's eat one more chocolate.
Tell me how many
more days till Christmas.

Tomorrow sweet child!
Don't peak at the gifts.

Dedicated To Human

There comes a time when humanity has to understand the simplicity factor of the earth we live in.

All the technology of the world has zero value if we don't have the need internally to convert and coexist at peace. Even a corporate scaling back may be needed.

Thousands of years ago like your forefathers from before, they would once hold their hands to their many Gods in the skies. This was the start, called the dawning of consciousness.

We too will one day raise our hands up to skies. The spirit of Kanat and betterment merged together is the birth of higher reasoning. An accession of the ills of past flights gone by.

Human Rights Centre Geneva

Dear God,

We will live humbly and at peace with our environments only to survive, and not try to amass anything.

We will all be educated and avoid primacy at the highest levels.
And acknowledge we may be bored.

Every living person will kneel to the laws of earth implemented as designed. That the laws of earth for all are supreme, a global bonding to just be better.

We will more effectively communicate the problems of land. And give our women birth control. While putting a value on human life. But most important we will acknowledge earth; it being our temporary holding cell and the signs to the skies on human rights day will read:

God we wish to boycott, sit and wait out this transition. A solemn pledge of brotherhood, how the thin shell of blood that you designed became human in spirit, how our world has agreed to become socially one for betterment now!

S34- Switzerland

Alp Is Still Thy Name

The green treetops produce dew.
Lethal are its peaks, thus
Alp became thy name.

"You are the mountain warrior",
us shamans once said.
For the many who lost lives
and the evil spirits you brought.
Even Asia couldn't touch your peaks.

Today so modern and pretty,
thousands of years later.
Geneva became their heart,
church bells replaced indigenous temples.
Many things have transformed.
Its people, its culture, its food.

One thing has not changed.
The green treetops still produce dew.
The mist of past settles on the
busy cities.

But Alp is still thy name.

Church By The Mountain

S35- Syria

One thousand years ago after a sacrifice was
made, the wish for betterment and healing was
done by praying to the Sky Gods.

Today we know better, that God just lets us be….

Hope

S36- Syria

The Shamans of Su'Riyah We the Akkad's emerged from Syria. Much of our tribes were killed, our settlements were brutally destroyed. Now we became the Akkads of the Sumer regions. Caspian our new territory and home. Our Semitic lead Sargon I was the one in control. The Tigris and Euphrates is the holy water we still enjoy.	Sargon I

— T —

Ilha Formosa – The Beautiful Island

We are the Malayo-Polynesian ancestry of the aboriginal population of Taiwan.

The following people have all lived on our island, the Portuguese, Han Chinese, Dutch, Spanish and Manchua Asians.

Our forefathers would say…

Hell is frightening, with the souls of the monstrous demons that exist.
Learn to always live at peace with the ones who come and stay.

The Flowers Of Taiwan

Tadzhik

We are the ancient people of Sogdians.
We have lived in these dense river networks for centuries.

From the outside we all look the same but even our own tribe can be subdivided into seven very distinct groups of people.

Most don't know but Sarazm is one of the earliest proto-urbanization trade areas of the region.
Why do you need to know this because our elders would say:

We have seen many faces, heard many stories but our ancestral bones still rattle in the sun, today.

Our Ancestral People

T3- Tanzania

Tan Tan Goes The Gods

Tan Tan the noises of lightening
goes the Gods,
mortified when they strike down.

Ban Ban is the food
that we feed them,
hoping they don't prey on us.

On On is the ten fingers in the skies
is our destined plight,
their weight heavy.

Tar Tar is the hail,
under the moon,
their spirits above us.

Always remembering the murmurs
of puffy clouds.
That we all came from indigenous
known as the headless discarnate beings.

Hit cover quick, when Tan Tan goes
the Gods.

Lightening And Noise Of Tan Tan Goes The
Gods

Spirits Of Past Life

Two thousand years ago the Caucasoid people from Southern Kushite Ethiopia moved into our land. Our tribal pressures began.

At around the same time the iron wielding Bantu people from Western Africa also moved in. They proudly eliminated most of our local tribes.

Everything was fine until the Portuguese came.

We then knew their spirited omens of our past ancestry had come back to cause havoc on the land.

Our people told the remaining part of them, it is because of your past actioms that tan tan now goes the Gods.

Mask Of Caucasoid Kushite People

T5- Thailand

Buddhism

Calm is our soul,
tranquility we find in nature.

We say to those lost,
put your hand in the mud and
feel the life in it.

Pick up the tiny worm,
in the mush of clay
and sense its soul move around.

Don't be disconnected
with earth.
That man made mounds of
concrete there to fool us.

Watch the life still move around,
It has a soul and a purpose,
understand the life within it.

We believe in a no kill policy for life.
The splendours of earth,
meant to connect us to human
from the divine.

Inside our homes.
We live with the bugs, scorpions and snakes.
Gently moving them from our paths.
Do you find our ways odd?

Your foods are that modified!
Your meat is packaged, hidden is
the torment to animal.
Heavy chemicals you use,
did you think they just disappeared?

They only come back to you
as a punishment from the skies.
Ironically we find your lack of quality
in life odd.

Mediate and understand earth
to feel linked to the skies.
It will heal you from the karma,
of injuring your own selves' in this cycle of life.

Child Holding worm

T6- Timor Leste

The Black Triangle

The power of many will crush any stupidity,
clans we will stay.

Let's battle these foreign and make them all go
away.

The black is the past omen of colonization;
the stars represent world peace at present day.

Heritage Symbols

T7- Togo

The Constant Of Vocal

Today we have literature, Ballet African du Togo
and Art. But our forefathers once had said.

Change is the only constant of the planet!
Albert Einstein would understand the Kwa
people's musical dialogues better today.

Eeee = mc ^{2}

Two Million Years Ago We Made Way

T8- Tonga

The Summit Of Volcano

Our rituals for the preparation of war are an
actual process.
Our men are blessed in tapa cloth made of bark
and weave.

We must first drink the K'ava pepper plant
with its mild narcotic.
Once at the summit of the Volcano, they
have to feed the female bitch in the sky.

Help us sing this tribal chant.

ma⊠ulu⊠ulu, ma⊠ulu⊠ulu,

How we would pray as we told them good-bye.

Young Coconut Jelly

Take the stone and crack
open the young coconut.
Drink its water and start
scooping out its mushy jelly.
Enjoy it slowly and heal your
brittle lips.

Then come join us,
darker skin you are.
Indian a lot of us are.

Trash bins we have made into
steel drums.
Day and night we beat on
to forget the impacts of
slavery and our own misery.

Now dance!
If you are still sad we may
put a little of the master's rum
in your jelly.

The Amphitheatre

Our elder has summoned
everyone!
He says this young man
is evil, at the first rainfall we
will sacrifice him.

Do not eat the poisonous plants.
You must feel the torment
otherwise the omen spirits
in you, will follow us back.

He died slowly screeching in pain.

His spirit from past life
returns to the very same spot
he was sacrificed.

This time the Romans are here.
They have replaced the
awkward stones.
And have opted to forgo this

shamanic site with
what looks like a colossal
structure.

They have name it the same though!
El-Jem is this structure's name.
For the laws of the first of the many
before them.
The only thing different other than the
size are the cages and what is
eaten today by lions.

It seems to be entertainment of
what was once done but in a more
advance way.

El Jem Amphitheatre

Hagia Sohia

A simple stone dolmen,
then a shamanic temple,
A church, today,
a transformed Mosque.

How you stand unbroken.
Magnificent is your splendour.
A renaissance of each era.

Aya Op Hi (hee)
When grunts were heard.
Did you wonder,
where their spirits went?
Or what was in the skies?

Saint Sohia
When Byzantium
church bells rang,
Did you hear the
howls of your earliest
forefathers?
The ones whose echo came
from the skies.

Aya Sofya
When songs of
Ottoman prayers
blared out on,
Ramadan day.
Did you hear,
the church bells chime
of our past.

Hagia Sohia I ask of you:
Who came, who left?
Reminiscent of our past.

Your ancient structure.
Sprits of time,
concepts of the many Gods.
Who have disappeared over time.

So much blood,
Yet we are one generation
to the next,
just a humble passage of time.

Continue…

<u>*Continue*</u>

In our indigenous hearts,
you will still be,
our ancient shamanic heritage.
Holy in wisdom
Aya Op he'ya

You stood the strongest test of time.

Christ In Hagia Sophia Today- The Moon And
The Spirits Aya Op Hi(hee)

T12- Turkey

The Hidden Underground

Derin Kuyu you are not the
only hidden.
Babel we cried out loud.
Don't fool us Gods,
anymore.

Oh lord, the damages we have
not knowingly done.
A million years of shamanic spoken
ancestry,
Holy in nature.
No more.

The written destroyed.
Past civilizations, and the lives
we harmed
No more.

Our hidden scripts, our ancestry
we now know.

Diagram is Derin Kuyu Turkey
(Hidden Underground City)

Isyanbul- Istanbul

Find torment, our battles ensued. During bloody clashes the ambassador in Constantinople was committed to the prison of the seven towers.

The seven became his lethal transposition of death. An omen that meant torture or consumption of what is afterlife. Yedi.

Merely a few centuries before the seven towers reflected the seven final and fatal mountain tips.

§

London, United Kingdom

We are civil and not like them they said. Evolve is our spirit. Even our dead will be delicately woven into our landscapes.

Today we will abandon the shamanic ritual of the past and simply call our graveyards the "Magnificent Seven".

A Gravestone At Nunhead, One Of The "Magnificent Seven" London Cemeteries.

The Victims, Of The End Of War

Priest, I am so young with two small children,
they killed my husband.
We are Assyrian and this holy church is the only
thing I trust.
A boy can save himself.
I am going to Syria to find my
distant relatives.

Please can you just take my son
Till I can get him back.

The Priest responds:
We don't really have a lot but this is a house of
God, we will try our best.
Distant relatives, I am so young with a
single daughter.
The age of her breast are so tender please can you
take her,
till I get back.

If a few other days go by,
you can marry her to anyone.
A very sad day for me, for the clan violence that
may occur to a foreign child alone with

them. This was our horrid family's faith.
Could this be better than death, I am desperate.
May she immediately produce a son to ease her
wounds, to blend in with them.

God in this remote Assyrian church I stand alone
in front of you.
Can you forgive me for the life I am
about to take.
You know the forbidden in our cultures.
I don't know how to read or write.
My husband is the only man who should touch
the divine.
My kids she wails; this was the best I could do.

The true story of a son who waited 70 years in
a church monastery in Southern Turkey for his
mother to come back.
Taken from Anatolian newspapers, a replicated
version to illustrate damages caused by war.

Educate, Some More?

Happily, I went to the market.
Sir may I say,
do you have some blueberries for
me in store today?

He came out and gave me
Raspberries, I said no.
Gooseberries, I said no.
Finally he said voila,
and showed up with the blackest
berries.

I said no.

He spent an half hour
or so,
he said madam a berry,
is a berry we got no more.
Why do you look so sore?

I said no.

Raspberries have brittle,
gooseberries have the bitterness of lead,
and black berries,
as sweet as they may be,
will not go with my scone I just made.

Sadly I turn to the exit door,
before I leave,
may I educate you some more?
A berry is not a berry,
This is not what I was looking for.

The blues are not red, green or black.
Lastly all these flavours to me
are allergic, and wack.
Sir may I say, I am not sore,
The blues were the only ones
I was simply looking for.

No Blue is Not a Red

Earthquake

The Gods are so mad
they cried.
Smoke is still spewing out
from its soil.
The earth has cracked
help us please.

We are transforming to human,
and just became humbled by the skies.
The grumbling of earth was so loud.
We are just starting to develop
consciousness.

The spirits did Jin, a form of
evil last night.
With us not knowing,
they were out in full disguise.

When we think about it.
Even beliefs were given
to us by the land and the seas.

We begged the different Gods to stop.
We have no clue,
why this has happened
to the innocence on earths as a being?

When the land moved,
there were so many gone.
We are still begging help
us please.

Split Soil Of An Earthquake

T17- Tuvalu

The Spanish Explorer

The Spanish explorer Alvaro de Mendana de
Neira in 1568 said:

Smell the air by the sea
and feel this mist coming
down from the sky.

The Lord has delicately
blended in everything
so beautifully.

Tuvalu and Kiribati
should be known as
the land of
singing birds,
coconut milk and
beautiful half naked
Polynesian women.

We are hoping all
of them submit and comply.

Kiribati Speaking Female

— U —

The Gods

I met all the Gods and they
had no color.
I met all the Gods and they
said we all have been moulded
from human designs.
I met all the Gods and they
whispered you are chosen.

I said to them but I am
a humble man from Bantu.
On this land I roam.
With waterbuck leather,
that is still stained with
dry blood on my back.

To others who asked
how I met all the Gods
I simply replied.

I merely looked at the moon
Over the, first Tombs of
Kings.

And simply saw them.

They even spoke to me.
I swore up and down,
I speak the truth.

Adamant I stand,
I met all the Gods.

I Meet All The Gods

Titanium

I am titanium made of an
unbroken will. But even
this strength sometimes fails to
go through the war.

On a cross that was meant
to lay.
The whips slash my body,
bloody becomes my soul.
My brain whispers through the torment.

Look at this ancient Forest,
and stay very still.
Hear their earliest noises.
Feel their spirits and don't fester.
You just got to ride the chi
of dark, a real life tester.

Let the eagle push
forth the power of wind.
Harness tightly its delicate
wings.

Start at zero,
wipe clean your gruesome past.
This pain beyond belief
that you thought permanent,
would surely not last.
This spell so obscure is really temporary.
Made from the dark clouds of
demonic evil exposed out from its sanctuary.

I now understand the concepts of life.
My existence has been made so great.
the titanium of my might.

Primeval Beech Forest

Evil Spirits

Evil has come to our region,
we had made into a home for centuries.
We carried an old aqueduct system at close to
4500 years.
We had a well, pottery, tombs and a Neolithic
enclosure, called our earliest settlements.

Our land and that of the neighbouring regions
became too violent. Food ran out.
We leave you behind Al Ain, an omen of past
time.
We have opted to settle in Baluchistan and will
rebuild. We will now even do the same type of
pottery.

The evil spirits got the best of our region and pray
these omen spirits to not follow us through.

The Evil Spirits Of Al Ain

Evolutionary Difficulties

They were ok with Charles Darwin, but they are not ok with me?

I stood in front of all the Royal Monarchs
And asked, "why can't you just let me be"?

I thought you favoured female leaders?
Don't you know shamans were once part of thee?

The century is 21ˢᵗ and this is also your lineage ancestry. Please try to see the depth of our human evolutionary tree?

I am aware in modifying Darwin; the world won't be same.
This was not guess work but rather the study of social theories meant for humans to gain.

I incorporated divine in all your pain.
It really isn't that hard if we simply understand.

*"One by one Gods children came.
All built by his loving hand.
In the end the equation is simple.
We were simply moulded to each section of earth as humans, let's try to be tame".*

What makes you different from them, is so easy to separate. Centuries later, you had royals, they just had breaking of sticks and bare feet to navigate.

The Lady With The Lamp

Florence Nightingale we
call upon you,
we will send you over
with a team of 25.
Help our British soldiers in need.

In Istanbul you will be stationed
with them.
On the Asiatic side, where are men
will desperately need your hand.

The conditions are so unsanitary,
more assistance is needed,
a telegraph goes back.

I have decided to keep notes.
More have actually die from non-battle
related wounds than the ones who came back
from the Crimean war.

The regions are horribly suffering.
Overcrowding is severe,
we do have cholera outbreaks.

I am implementing organization
to the best of my ability.

We are trying to be human and
save all.

Nightingale In Istanbul, Turkey

U6- United Kingdom, England

The Light of Europe

Early in the 1800's,
at the height of its empire.
The British Dominion looked
beyond the seas.
They supported the base of Oxford
and knew to be progressive it had to be
strengthen.

Call it our interesting past.
The many Dukes and Duchess',
the irony of their vision of civility
that wanted to last.
Henry Morton Stanley, Henry Godwin,
and, Hugh Gough, to name just the few Sirs.

They said lets intricately study these
primitive foreign, make all their blood smear.
Merged secret alliances.
The treaties, of the many misunderstood
shamanic conceptions.
Bloodshed after bloodshed,
many enemies made them fear.

Out came enlightenment,
to the world they presented.

Little is advertise, how being better
at the time than the rest of the territories
that continuously attack.
Made them so Barbar resented.

Long hidden was their records of origin.
North Africa to Caucasus, we utter today.
Hey wait a minute Europe
that was your ancestral forefather's way.

*Humanity don't ever look cynical at our historical
past.*

When dark clouds of time comes, and
The Dominion enters hungry, the vast lands.
The question then posed was "my clan or yours",
only one can last.

The light of Europe shone.

The Light

U7- United Kingdom

Cock-Fighting

I am the Baron Rothschild Lionel of The East
Indian Company, you need to entertain my team
and I.

Alpha Quadrant

Once upon a time, when land was not owned.
Caucasians lived in China and Asians in Europe.
Does this throw you off?

This is a true story in "defining human" of one
researcher huff!
When the planet said that humans came from
different sources. A correction was thought
through.

These poems were written while under house
arrest for telling academics understand clans
for monkeys their dialogues is really something
pertaining to all of you.

As numbers grew and darks clouds of time
drew in. The land, became dominated.
Called a controlled territory this is how the story
of unravelling all sorts of radicalization really
begins.

§

Once upon a time, indigenous lived in Africa,
but the same indigenous also lived in America.
Does this throw you off?

Columbus this time got confused and lumped all
of them as shamanic Indian fools.
This is a true story regarding the difficulty one
person had in explaining social variation through
the simplest use, of the many fruits and berries.
Oh the ridicule.

§

Once upon a time, more like a handful of years
ago. North Africa to Anatolia was 600 years of
one massive Ottoman linguistic pool.
Does this throw you off?
This is when no countries existed only a Sultan
or two.
Do you know how all this research pass
through?
I had to distribute my work for not being
academic enough while I explained to them
genetics, revolution of stars and how I could be
the king's fool.
Star trek was visionary and futuristic you may
or may not believe but in the end the world of
technology, information and what is the Borg
will be the very real analogy.

Kokopelli Tribe

To the sky's we blow a kiss.
Do you know us?
Root to skies we would say;

Kok or Gok
Gok or Kok

The dances of our forefathers,
feathers that are in disarray.
The symbol of fire.
Earthy spirits from terra,
lift us to the skies.

Kok or Gok
Gok or Kok

Blood we smear,
Nails we leave long.
Each scratch represents,
the number who have
died.

Kok or Gok
Gok or Kok

Skip around with might,
We do sounds for our dead.
Happy always is our tribe

Kokopelli today translated from Anatolia to across Central Turkic-Asian countries means:

"Kiss God's hand"

Native Kokopelli

The Other Side Of War

The struggle of human
is beyond belief.
The dry arid and painfully,
harsh deserts.

Our benefits at a
brutal cost.
The other side
that no one sees.

Giving benefits to those
on its own soil,
is as old as the first humans
that were born.

Give us moral and faith.
Stop fighting the same
team.
Everything you have is
because of a soldier's hope.

Behind the clouds,
a metal tag and a uniform outfit.
Given with such heartache.

A mother's wish and tears
for a better country.

U11- United States

Stuck At The Border

Mr. Officer I swear to you
I am innocent.
What's the big deal
They are only files
from a 100 years' old.

Linguistic anthropology
and technology.
What can I say?

They surrounded me with might.
I nibbled on my Smarties.
Want some? I teased?

Guess what Canada has
nothing that big,
I will fight for it back
vigilantly.
All these files belong to me.

I am better now.
Can you show some
neighbourly love?
I know competition is your way
But this one is all of ours.
Please can there be no foul play.

U12- United States

Apache

Nomadic plains we travel.
Our language belongs to
the Athabaskan group.

We say one thing to the
white man only:

From man and women appeared both our worlds.

Apache's Circle

Manhattan

Once upon a time
before the Empire State
building,
before the lights
and all the concrete.

There lived for centuries American
Natives on its soil.
They left many recipes, artefacts and
heritage things for settlers.
Most were claimed by others.

But their forefather's spirits in the skies kept
calling on earth,
the bones of our ancestral past.
Continuously praying for these
un-rested souls.

Just when humanity eradicated
everything due to our primitive past.
Scriptures were found so holy
even the biggest could not
cover the existence of the reminders
of their earliest cues.

They had no written but a
volcano of history may have
erupted with what was about to
be told.
  The names, of certain regions.
  One that connects
  the heart to the spirit
  pounding in the skies.
  We are here and still breathing,
  but you can't see us.
  The force of what is living is our
  descriptive reminders,
  of those that were unsaved.

How shall the unsaved ones escape back to the
heavens? The skies use to say.
If they are stuck between the earth and the
heavens.
Their neglected souls release should be
humanities "greatest of salvations".

Of that which was once done.
Our confusion regarding our hidden past.

Their protectorate of respect to the land and
no domination, an epoch of years of peaceful
existence.

An attempt by some to cover the sun
with clay for a temporary disguise.
So many generation of children.
The years that had all gone by.

These spirits continue their prayers.
Follow us we are here to guide you now, on the
eve of a warm summer celebration day they sent
wings from the skies.
  "Learn from those who
  have not rested.
  Make amends with spirits
  of what is living around you".
  Let them break you free.

Unwell will become the people and the land,
our human connection to life, should be what is
in command.

Living is what we use to walked on.
This will start to transform its original
colors back to green from grey.

Learn the h-at-tan way. Another word for
beating life, of our Native spiritual ways.

U14- United States, Los Angeles

I Am The Fallen Angel Lucifer

I want to be free,
free of any demise of even righteousness.
I want pleasure all the time.
I hate everything that is bound
by the laws of God.

I enjoy all the benefits that the darkness designs.
Why do they try to box me or loathe me?
Not understanding the power of the obscure
within me.
They have clipped my wings and I now
walk in human form.

I am the fallen angel Lucifer in disguise.

Lucifer With His Team

U15- Uruguay

The Poisonous Shells

Oh spirits
The waters are so blue.
The land is so warm.
Yet we suffer so much.

Our ancestry use to say:

*"when sickness reaches and
destitute you have become"*

At low tide
go to the shores.

Find the poisonous shells.
The ones we dry out delicately,

with palm sticks and use for
décor.

And reincarnate without pain
back to earth for better more.

The Many Poisonous Shells

The Moon In The Day

I saw the white moon in the day
and asked, *"why did you shed your lunar color?"*

He responded, "it is to transcend further
down towards the clouds and match
their surroundings."

We came closer by climbing Nurata
and continued, *"why don't you join us here on
earth, the leading light you are?"*

The moon said "At 93 million miles, the distance
to go back home would be far too great.
Its spirit must stay high, the light is the sensation
we wish to give the eyes and most importantly
we are the ones that can emit colour?"

We will simply stay in our planetary system
and you can use us when darkness falls and no
other lights are there to help you.

The White Moon

— V —

| **Chief Roi Mata**

It does not matter how slowly I went,
or the pain I felt upon departing.
What matters is my eternal existence. | Roi |

| **Homage To The Sky**

Oh Atheist Oh Atheist
How do you not believe in thee?
See
The glass butterfly,
its protective wings made transparent.
Delicately glass blown by
the heavens above.

Hear
Oh Atheist Oh Atheist
how do you not heart thee?
The ocean waves
lashing on the shores
releasing sounds through vibrations
of those living in it.

Speak
Oh Atheist Oh Atheist
how do you not sense thee?
The internal organs of man
its life grown from specks of
earth, in a shell of blood
over thousands of years. | The hovering of air puff clouds,
a peacock's tulle crown or
a pink river dolphin.

My soul pours out to you,
how do you not even consider in thee?

Peacock's tulle crown |

Caracas

The dark mountains we twirl around
the winding roads to the top.
The glassmaker sits patiently.
An indigenous trade-maker
heats the crystals carefully.
Out comes the blown glass.

He says "what would you like
me to make for you"?
Please sir pick anything.
Teach me everything
you know!

Well he blows gently and a spiral
of some sort of hot figurine
comes out.
Once upon a time
our elders also created art.

This form I built with my
hands may mean nothing
to you but it houses the spirits
of our first chiefs.

They once lived between tributaries
at the base of the mountains.
Their only fears were the visits
they would have to make.
Called the dark force of the mountain tops.

Etched in design we kept their
different figurines made from
the land, close to us.

Take this back to Canada.
He lifts the figurine outside the
shed he works in,
and looks at the sky of the mountain.

I just called for their spirits.
To be instilled in the glass.
It will protect you.
No money needed.
For remembering to preserve our history.
It is a gift from me to you.

Caracas Mountain Hilltop

Listen Only To Your Inner Soul

Vietnam also has an eye
in the sky, it watches them.
It says follow your conscious,
The delicate Feng shui principles,
your inner soul.

The voice of reason,
the thoughts of moral.
Nothing out beats
that of your divine purpose.

In the dark that voice
speaks to you.
God is you and your inner
soul.

Listen To Your Inner Soul

Al- Yaman

An ancient culture, parked in the shores
by the Red sea.

They eventually made San'a their fortified
place, a region at an altitude of 2,200m.
Situated in a mountain valley.

The few camel skin tent that were covered
with greenery as camouflage for
those who may attack, was blended in.

At night there only entertainment
was sitting around a small fire
and recalling stories of old
proverbs, superstitions, mysticism
and poetry centuries old.

But even before trade took place
with the Babylonians and Egyptians.
Or the Islamic nomads of Arabia,
Jews or Shi'a from Persia
had move in.

They fed angrily the spirits of
those before them.
To the bastardized Gods they
would ululate and screech.

This one is for you.

Al- Yahman

The Highest

The ancient doors.
The one whose light
shines glory.
We ask to be salvaged.

The womb in the sky responds,
Venus are the Gods,
A battle of lost, you seem to have endured
on earth the say.
What makes you wonder?

Twist of power has given way
based on the hardship of land,
the women say.

Horrid pain we feel.
We fight the realm
of struggle.
War leaves us destitute in appeal.
Deprivation, from the region of
Baal.

Ana, mother of all supreme.
Our confusion is unbearable.
We were the ones that created,
the lineage of concubines
of ancestry.
How we continued life, century after century,
why is this happening to thee?

Dark clouds continuously cover,
the seven mountainous tips.
The green gardens of the heaven
turned over all our keys.

Poverty has taken the better of us.
Covenant to God is no longer
part of us.
Send down a male, this time.
He will be God's child.
Power we will have to relent.
We will grab the children
and hope his wisdom can protect us.
A servitude of that to be reconciled.
Dark Female Venus

Kariba

Our God is a black female.
Also once made from the region
where women went to
consummate the marriage.

Her blood that once dripped told us,
their ancestry is now our ancestry.
The importance of the ones that
give life.

The tribal brothers would say:

We make them compete so our
children become fierce.
We make them jealous so
our men get the best care.

And lastly we pray to them when
they died, our acknowledgement
that we are aware of their
spirits in the sky.

The Garden Region Of Consummation

We Were Born Ilk-hans
(Inside Our Family)

I think of my ancestral departed, the irony of a discovery that links the meaning of the first of the family, to the wings of past gone.

Out of Africa came the shamanic word Kan, the earliest meaning of the blood of our ancestry.
Out of Anatolia and Early Asia came Kan-at.
The wings that drew blood, the evil Jin of our forefathers.

Out of India came the Khans
An abbreviation of Khanat, as the spirits in lead.
Out of Israel, the wings throughout the holy lands from before, became their songs of Gush (kush).

Fifty thousands years ago Canada also had Kanats, but this time a protected" spiritual wing cover,
became a completely different change in cultural tune.
But it was out of Mongolia,
Genghis Khan who merged
his kingdom in four and

taught me history,
by far the most.

Call it the spirits of their past voice. He said we rule as a mighty, of all the territories we claim.

The Khans of East Asia, merge them with the Khanat's of Turkestan and that of Khanat's of Persia, lastly let the Khanat's of the Golden Horde join in.
These are our wings of our historical past.
But it was my grandpa who once said:

One hundred years ago, we picked Ilk-hans, as the first of the family, these are the clans of our own heritage to represent an ancestral gift for generations of you.

ABOUT THE AUTHOR

Born in Zeynep Kamil Hospital in Istanbul, Turkey and of Canadian heritage since the age of one, Yildiz Ilkin has presented this work for pushing social betterment by gluing her years of hobby research on many various academic subjects.

All which are and will be presented under the label of progressive environmentalism.

The following poems were done under grueling house confinement and relatively quickly.
The objective being to convince with legal might that we have not reach our better evolutionary plateau due to human invasiveness and mismanagement on land. Therefore, if there are any comments, questions, historical edits etc. you can email her at ventingroom@yahoo.com.
Please note. The study notes for it can be found in her research center on www.starilkin.com at a later date.
Other Pages Of Interest www.vancats.com

Art Gallery
www.oceanus12.wix.com/thefuture

Printed in the United States
By Bookmasters